The Politically Incorrect Guide® to
Science Fiction
and Fantasy

The Politically Incorrect Guide® to
Science Fiction
and Fantasy

D. J. Butler

Since 1947
REGNERY

An Imprint of Skyhorse Publishing, Inc.

Regnery books may be purchased in bulk at special discounts for sales promotion, corporate gifts, fund-raising, or educational purposes. Special editions can also be created to specifications. For details, contact the Special Sales Department, Regnery Publishing, 307 West 36th Street, 11th Floor, New York, NY 10018 or info@skyhorsepublishing.com.

Regnery® is a registered trademark of Skyhorse Publishing, Inc.®, a Delaware corporation.

Visit our website at skyhorsepublishing.com.
Please follow our publisher Tony Lyons on Instagram @tonylyonsisuncertain.

10 9 8 7 6 5 4 3 2 1

Library of Congress Cataloging-in-Publication Data is available on file.

Jacket design by Jason Sunde
Cover image by Shutterstock

Print ISBN: 978-1-68451-541-7
eBook ISBN: 978-1-944824-34-1

Printed in the United States of America

CONTENTS

CONTENTS

Introduction

WHAT IS GOING ON HERE?

What is this book, and what is it not?

First of all, there's probably a word missing from the title if we were striving for real accuracy. This book should perhaps be called *The Politically Incorrect Guide to Science Fiction and Fantasy Literature*. The book contains numerous sidebars and verbal asides on points relating to SFF literature: sidebars about movies and television, about gaming, about nerd culture, about conventions, fandoms, and the various organizations that make up the sociality surrounding SFF literature, about graphic art, and many other things. However, this book is above all else a book about books. Not only is it about books, but it is principally about novels.

Second, I should confess right up front that this book makes no attempt to be encyclopedic. Encyclopedias of the subject matter do exist.[1] They are big and bulky, informative, but not entertaining. Similarly, this book makes no claim to be objective. You can say objective things about literature, but those things aren't interesting: the word count and date of first publication won't feed your soul. Instead, this book is deeply rooted in my perspective, which the editors at Regnery have reason to think might be sufficiently politically incorrect for their purposes (perhaps it was my publication of a short story entitled "The Seven Nipples of Molly Kitchen"?). Really, what I'm telling you here in the first page of the introduction is that the title is entirely wrong. If we were being strictly descriptive, this book would be called *Dave's Guide to Science Fiction and Fantasy Novels*.

In order to tell you what I want to tell you about science fiction and fantasy, though, I am going to tell you some unvarnished truths. In a literature that is creative and open to expressing a wide range of ideas, some of the ideas expressed are pernicious. Moreover, one of the themes you'll see over the course of the book is that science fiction and fantasy literature has been produced by communities. Those communities have produced many extraordinary characters, and maybe more than their share of predators. This is not a harmless literature. It pays to go into it with your eyes open, and it pays to have your eyes open when your kids are reading it, too.

But third, the phrase science fiction and fantasy is . . . complicated. At the very least, it bears some explaining.

What Is Fantasy?

Fantasy is the older literature here, so we'll take it as our starting point.

The roots of fantasy are deep. We're going to talk about ways in which fantasy is rooted in the earliest literature of the species and even earlier, in the wordless representations we left painted on cave walls tens of thousands of years ago when we were allegedly bands of inbred cannibals hunkering our way through an ice age. But in fact, the roots of fantasy are deeper still than that. The roots of fantasy literature are in the parts of human experience and the human mind that we cannot see.

There are various ways to talk about this, and I will try several. First, let's start with the neurological way.

Our brains evince various kinds of structure, including a division into right and left hemispheres. When I was young, we were told that the left brain was analytical, and the right brain was creative. (Since each hemisphere was said to govern the hand on the opposite side of the body, this was why left-handed people were more creative, my tenth-grade Health teacher informed me, to the mortification of my right-handed soul aspiring to creativity.) This bears enough relationship to the truth to be persuasive, but neurologists have refined the picture in the, ahem, decades since I was young. The difference between the hemispheres is that the left brain and the right brain distribute focus differently.

The left brain focuses narrowly. It looks at the problem at hand, at the table of columns, at the road in front of the car. In fact, it's not even really looking at the apparent object of its focus—instead, it's looking at an abstraction of the idea or object it apparently focuses on. The left brain considers only a model of a narrow slice of reality.[2]

Does that sound a little scary? You're driving down the road, watching the asphalt ahead whipping toward you at approximately ten miles per hour faster than the posted speed limit, and your brain isn't even focused on what it sees up there. Instead, it's focusing on *a model it has built of the road ahead*.

But your left brain has to be focusing on a model or you wouldn't be able to drive. Your left brain is taking not only the visual and other sensory data you're getting in the moment in which you barrel down the freeway, but also vast amounts of information you've collected over time as a driver and otherwise, to supplement the visual data with information about depth perception and distance, weather and its likely effect on the surface of the road, and other inputs, to create an artificial model, a simulation of the real world that you use to drive.

Yes, you definitely are living in a simulation, or at least you are constantly moving through a simulation. It's the one built by your own left brain.

The left brain focuses narrowly, and what it focuses on is not the real thing(s), but a model of the real thing(s). This makes the left brain really good at solving puzzles. That focus on an abstraction of the problem is where we as a species go to solve a Rubik's cube, devise a new tool for an engineering problem, do math problems, etc.

The right brain, by contrast, focuses on everything. Everywhere. All at once, to borrow a phrase. The right brain is where identity lives, because identity is a cluster of relationships between us and other people, or between us and things or groups, or between us and the past. We see this in the way we introduce people. "This is Dave, Emily's husband. He works at the Stouffer's plant. You remember him, he's the guy who got drunk at last year's Christmas party and fell face-down in the egg salad." Our right brain perceives all the relationships and knows the identity of things.

Another way to say that is that our right brain knows meaning.

The basic difficulty is that our left brain can't look into our right brain. Our right brain sees everything all at once, but as They Might Be Giants sang, it's "where your eyes don't go." We have a part of us that knows everything we know, and it's the part we can't consciously access.

Fantasy literature is the art that uses the ancient tools of primal man to access what is in the right brain. All literature can do this, but fantasy in particular has held on to the tried, true, trusted and original tools. Those tools are many. Analogy and metaphor are a case of tools used by the fantasy novelist. The fantasy writer uses Archetype as a tool, and therefore his stories abound in heroes, princesses, and monsters (and can be derided by critics as cliché). Storytelling structure is a tool of the fantasy novelist, as is surprise.

However, magic is one of the greatest tools of fantasy storytellers. As we discuss below, magic is a difficult idea to pin down, but it lives on the shadowy borders of the right brain, the archetypal, the anthropological, the instinctual. Somewhere between science and religion or maybe undergirding both, magic crouches with its web of occult connections, its analogies of microcosm and macrocosm, and its laws of sympathy and contagion. It has no desire to entertain us; it wants to show us how to get things done. It is the knowledge that provides power, and power in this case to drive stories closer to the cave of ancient loot, the human right brain.

Other kinds of literature explore the right brain too, but fantasy, by embracing magic, monsters, and the gods, picks up the tried and true toolkit of the plains shaman, the chanter in the kiva, and the oil-streaked hierophant, which give the fantasy writer great powers of vision. Except that the fantasy novelist may achieve visions herself or, like any artist, may fail to achieve insight consciously herself but may generate a tool for generating insights in the reader. Umberto Eco famously said that a novel was a "machine for generating interpretations,"[3] warning us that the interpretations are for the readers and the critics, and the novelist himself should write the book and then get out of the way. A fantasy novel is a machine for generating visions—and the vision does not belong to the author.

Great golden treasures lie hidden in the darkness of the right brain. What can those visions be about? The visions that result from the making of true and unexpected connections in the right brain are about identity and meaning. They are literally the structure of the perceived universe, even the unconsciously perceived universe, which makes them potentially cosmic or cosmological insights. If religion is the social exploration of questions such as who are we, why are we were, and what should we do, then fantasy literature at its best is frankly religious. It is not the religion of the pulpit but the religion of the prophet, the ecstatic, vision-generating utterance of the madman.

"Wait, wait," you cry. "This can't be right. You mean like . . . *Game of Thrones*? I'm supposed to think that's metaphysical literature? I thought it was just adventure stories about guys with swords!"

Ah. Well, you're not totally wrong. You've hit upon what we might think of as the bookseller's definition of the genre. When the bookseller unboxes a shipment of volumes from the publisher, he has to figure out where to put each volume on the shelf. The publisher helps the bookseller out (and also helps the browsing shopper) by printing on the cover that the book is FANTASY (or MYSTERY or whatever), and also designs and prints a cover that looks like it belongs on the FANTASY shelf. If you see a man with a sword fighting a dragon on the cover of a book, what genre do you think it belongs in? The bookseller or the casual reader might think about genre in terms of its external trappings, i.e., this book contains monsters and people casting spells, so it's a fantasy novel.

A Rabbi of SFF Literature might call this the peshat level of understanding, i.e., the obvious, surface level. And it's fine, as far as it goes. But, as we'll see, sometimes the surface trappings suggest one genre and the actual contents of the book suggests another. Beyond the surface level, fantasy is the what-if literature of the human spirit. This is why fantasy endures, not because of swords or chainmail. It has proved an enduring genre because it uses ancient tools. In the same way that tables have proved useful for thousands of years and we can therefore expect tables to continue to be around for thousands of more years, stories of gods and monster have proved useful for millennia, so they're not going away anytime soon.[4]

What Is Science Fiction?

Fantasy is the what-if literature of the human spirit. Science fiction is the what-if literature of human technology.

"But hold on," you say, raising a hand to stop me. "We agreed that, on a surface level, fantasy stories are stories about people hitting monsters with swords, right? So can't science fiction just be stories about people with ray guns and spaceships?"

Yes. But.

Yes, at the simplest, broadest level, at the level of "What shelf in the bookstore does this book go on?", science fiction means stories about people with ray guns and spaceships. But this genre, like fantasy, also proves it has legs,[5] so there must be something that gives it force and vitality other than just the flashiness of ray guns and the glamor of racing hovercraft against tentacled aliens in a desert arena.

Humans are toolmakers. We might not be uniquely toolmakers[6] but we're good at making and using tools. Making and using tools are characteristically human activities, they are tasks wherein our advantage over other species lies. As a form of literature, Science fiction characteristically asks "How might things be different with different (better) technology?" "What might the universe be like if we had tool or technology or capability X, which we do not now have?"

"Dave, that's dumb," you counter. "*Star Wars* is the most popular science fiction franchise of all time. What technology is it about? Hyperspace? The Force? Are you talking about the Force, Dave?"

Some of you have seen this coming, so let's have the moment. Star Wars, you see . . .

Drum roll.

. . . is not science fiction.

Of course it isn't science fiction. It's about space wizards, for crying out loud. Take out the Force and replace it with Magic and you'll see that Star Wars is a kind of fantasy. (Replace Magic again, this time with Faith, and you'll see that Star Wars is deeply religious.) At the peshat level (the SFF Rabbi nods), sure, Star Wars is science fiction. In the bookstore, if science fiction and fantasy are two separate shelves, the clerk probably slaps Star Wars into sci fi. But Star Wars is about space wizards mastering spiritual power, so in its heart, it isn't science fiction at all, ray guns notwithstanding.

Even on the peshat level, what you probably call Star Wars in a conversation with any reasonably nerdy reader isn't science fiction, in fact. You probably call it space opera. Space opera means big, melodramatic adventure stories with spaceships in them.[7] Battlestar Galactica is also

Sci Fi

The shortened moniker "sci fi" is thought to have been coined by writer, editor, and agent Forrest J. Ackerman in the 1950s. It echoed the then-cutting-edge term "hi-fi."

space opera (also arguably fantasy). Buck Rogers and Flash Gordon are space opera.

What are examples of science fiction, then? Consider Larry Niven's novel *Ringworld*, which explores the technological question, could you artificially engineer a planet that wasn't a sphere, but was instead a ribbon? If that ribbon circled around its star at the approximately the distance at which Earth orbits the sun, what are the logical consequences? The real heart of *Ringworld* is not the (fairly perfunctory) escapades of the crew of adventurers sent to explore the Ringworld when it's discovered, but the idea of the technology itself.

Famously, after publishing *Ringworld*, Niven was confronted by MIT students at the 1971 World Science Fiction Convention chanting "The Ringworld is unstable!" Their objection was not about the sociological setups of the story-world, but about the physics. Niven heard them out, agreed with their scientific and engineering analysis, and wrote a sequel to explain why, despite initial appearances, the Ringworld was stable after all.[8]

Another science fiction novel is Andy Weir's *The Martian*. The story is an adventure tale (the main character is a near-future astronaut left stranded on Mars), but the real concern of the book isn't to vividly describe blows, wounds, karate maneuvers, etc., or to follow twists and turns in human relationships, but to accurately explore the question, how could an astronaut stranded on Mars in fact survive until NASA was able to return to get him?

Famously, Weir tested his scientific and engineering ideas by crowdsourcing the technical criticism to the Internet.[9] Also famously, he failed to sell his novel to traditional publishing, which was convinced that no one would be interested in reading a story that was so focused on the technical details of the science and engineering, so he self-published his chapters as blog entries.[10] (Traditional publishing, like Hollywood, is comprised of pack animals. They run on conventional wisdom and buy in trends.) Somewhat less famously, it turns out that eventually, as we learned more about Mars, some of the crowdsourced answers Weir included in *The Martian* turned out to be false (the movie added further inaccuracies).[11] That is to say that science fiction, like true experimental science,[12] tends to falsify over time.[13]

This is not a bug, it's a feature. In fact, science fiction participates in scientific and technological development. I'm talking about big technologies, like artificial intelligence, self-driving cars, military tanks, virtual reality, submarines, solar sails, space stations, cloning, and the Internet, all of which were predicted by science fiction writers. But I'm also talking about the smaller, ubiquitous technologies they anticipated, like mobile phones, television, smart watches, holograms, video calls, drones, 3D printing, machine translation, and radar guns.[14] Did the writers predict the technologies because they were smart, and therefore prepare us for their advent? Maybe. Did the writers inspire entrepreneurs and engineers to create the technologies in their visions? Maybe there's some of that, too.

Science fiction is part of the intellectual skunk works of our civilization's technological and scientific development. It's the part where creative writers spin out imaginative concepts about technologies that might be, and what consequences would follow, packaged inside what are ostensibly adventure stories. Some of those ideas never come to fruition, and even the ones that do eventually become obsolete. But the whole is part of the scientific and technological conversation of modern times.

Other What-Ifs and a Broader Name

A third what-if literature gets recognized by name in publishers' catalogs and writers' biographies but generally doesn't get its own shelf in the bookstore. Alternate history is the genre that asks what-if questions about human history. What if John Wilkes Booth had missed? What if Hitler had continued to pursue the Allied forces at Dunkirk? What if Elizabeth I had married one of her favorites and produced a child? Alternate history has generally not been as popular as science fiction or fantasy (the popularity ranking goes like this: fantasy > science fiction > alternate history), maybe because its suppositions and insider jokes are most accessible to people who have a stronger grasp on history than the average reader.

Arguably, there is a fourth what-if literature (arguably there are more than that, but we'll stop at four for now). Some books ask what-if questions about human society. In other words, what if we organized society differently? What if we turned institution X on its head, or what if we extrapolated societal trend Y to its extreme? Most famously, this is true about dystopian literature, like George Orwell's *1984* or Aldous Huxley's *Brave New World*, or like the spate of dystopian novels that recently invaded young adult literature, spearheaded by Suzanne Collins with *The Hunger Games*. Historically, however, this literature has included unironic utopian works, such as Tommaso Campanella's *The City of the Sun* and Francis Bacon's *New Atlantis*,[15] which means there's a broader genre here than "dystopia," and the genre lacks a name.

If we were to coin a label for this broader genre, I'd propose allotopia or allotopic books. "Topia" just means "place" in Greek. "Ou" means "not," so a "utopia" is a place that doesn't exist, a place too good for the real world. "Dys" means "bad," so a "dystopia" is a bad place. "Allos" means "other," so an allotopia would be a novelistic exposition of a place that is different from here in some (social) respect, without prejudging whether that difference makes the described place superior or inferior.

Another kind of allotopia is the lost world story, in which the hero discovers a pristine land or an ancient civilization that has escaped the notice of the modern world by being hidden in a remote desert, or on an isolated plateau, or in the interior of the planet. Examples of this genre in book and film include H. Rider Haggard's *King Solomon's Mines*, Edgar Rice Burroughs's *Pellucidar*, the TV show *Land of the Lost*, the lost-world Western *Against a Crooked Sky*, and the delightfully illustrated *Dinotopia*.

Defining Genre: Science Fiction vs. Fantasy, and All the Other Ones

Genre is a bookseller's problem; genre is a way to communicate a package of expectations to the reading public. Books sitting together on a shelf labelled "Romance" or "Thrillers" have a predictable set of characteristics in common. Though Science Fiction and Fantasy have been and continue to be the mainstay genres of speculative fiction, there have been others.

The third great speculative genre is Horror. Horror is a genre that, distinctly from Science Fiction and Fantasy but in common with humorous writing and pornography, aims to elicit a physiological reaction from the reader. In the case of horror, this is the hair standing up on the back of the reader's neck or the sick feeling in the pit of the reader's stomach that something is not right. Horror is arguably an intrinsically moral genre to the extent that one of its great themes is that the universe is run by laws and when mankind breaks those laws there are terrible consequences. Philosopher of conservatism Russell Kirk wrote ghost stories, perhaps in part for this reason, or perhaps also because ghost stories carry within them a "deep sense of the past."[16]

Other genres express subsets of Science Fiction or Fantasy literature. Fantasy genres include Sword & Sorcery, Grimdark (see p. 137), Paranormal Romance and Urban Fantasy (see pp. 122), and arguably Steampunk (see p. 97). Science Fiction genres have included Planetary Romance (sometimes also called Sword & Planet; recounting adventures on exotic alien planets; the stories may not may not include spaceships), Cyberpunk (see p. 87), and Dystopian (see p. 109). Few of these have risen to sell such volumes that booksellers have dedicated whole sections or even shelves exclusively to their works. The Sword & Sorcery novels have generally lurked alongside Urban Fantasy, and sometimes even on the same shelves as Cyberpunk.

In today's bookstores, alternate history and utopias and dystopias (both of which typically lack the trappings of fantasy) are generally shelved either with science fiction or general literature. Suzanne Collins and her imitators are, of course, shelved with YA.

There is an umbrella term that covers all these genres, their subgenres, and for good measure, any other genres close to them that we may have missed. That term is "speculative fiction" or "spec fic." Any novel speculates, of course—it makes up characters, events, and/or places and then considers the consequences—but that's not what we mean. A novel that speculates beyond that to larger questions, a novel that asks what-if questions about the human spirit, human society, technology and tools, human history, or other major aspects of human existence, is speculative fiction.

Joining the Conversations

To ask a what-if question is to participate in a conversation, either by initiating the discussion or by way of response to someone else. Speculative fiction novels are a dialog. They want to dialog with each other, and also with you. The authors are in the conversation also, but separately from the novels. Once the author writes the book and sends it out into the world, the novel exists independently of its creator, whether the creator steps aside or not.

So there are conversations going on, built around these genres of literature (and in film, television, and games, as discussed elsewhere). These conversations are about ultimate things, like the nature of the universe and how we know things and how we approach life. And you are invited to join the conversation.

Throughout this book, I am going to touch briefly on a fairly long list of books and writers. This is not an exhaustive presentation of all the writers of speculative fiction, but it presents the headliners, the biggest names. For the most recent years, I've demurred to talk about very many individuals, but I've touched instead on some broad trends that I think define recent and current speculative fiction.

With this book, I want to invite you to join the conversation as a reader. I believe this literature has value. Speculative fiction is an imaginative part of the field notes of the human species. This work represents creative humankind struggling with its place in the cosmos, and it contains deep thoughts and works of great beauty.

I also want you to join the conversation in other ways. These field notes contain mistakes and also great blotches of human ugliness, lows that contrast starkly with the peaks. The field can benefit from your criticism. Share, praise, and teach the works that are good. The social manifestation of speculative fiction, fandom, can benefit from your participation, too. Come join us in building institutions that value and promote what is good in speculative fiction.

And consider the possibility that your experiences and ideas may be worth embodying in literature. Consider joining us as a writer.

Chapter One

PREHISTORIC AND EARLY FANTASY

The roots of fantasy literature run deep, and we can only scrape the surface here.

You will find that when you look up some of the writers in this chapter (Dunsany, Morris, and MacDonald, I'm looking at you), they are simply described as "fantasy" writers. Why am I putting them in this chapter with a discussion of cave paintings? Think of this as the chapter that breezily tries to summarize "what fantasy literature looked like before there was a Fantasy section in the bookstore."

From Cave Paintings to the Greeks

In 1940, a young man named Marcel found a hole in the ground under the roots of a toppled tree in south central France. Marcel was accompanied by his dog, who was named, delightfully, Robot. When Marcel realized that the hole opened into a larger cave, he left and came back with three friends to explore.

What the young men found was a cave complex whose walls were decorated with some 6,000 prehistoric images. The art of the Lascaux Cave, as it came to be called (it's in the Lascaux Valley, near the Lascaux Manor), is believed to be paleolithic, something like 18,000 years old. It includes images of recognizable species that are still around, like horses, but also identifiable species that have gone extinct, like Megaloceros (an extinct species of deer, sometimes called "Irish elk"). Famously, it includes a scene of a bison looming over a man lying on his back. The prone man has an erection;[1] this is strange enough, since he appears to be about to be trampled. Stranger, though, is that he also apparently has the head of a bird.[2]

What do we make of this? It's difficult to know. Our modern tendency is to write our own understanding over everything we see in the ancient world, and when we have run out of modern understanding to attribute, we call whatever's left "religion." I am willing to stipulate that "religion," broadly understood, is likely involved. What seems inescapable is that a human artist saw meaning connecting a bison with a prone man (sleeping? dead? waiting for the embrace of the bison?). The man is also a bird. And something about this bird-man encountering the bison was connected in the artist's mind with an erect phallus. Is this a sequence of images connecting to fertility? To effectiveness? To youth?

South of Lascaux, near the Spanish border, lies another cave, the Cave of the Trois-Frères, named for the three brothers who discovered it in 1914 with their father (who was not named Robot, but the Comte Henri Begouën). This cave is also full of prehistoric art which is dated to around 13,000 BC (about 3500 years before Göbekli Tepe was inhabited), and it also includes an image of an animal-man hybrid.[3]

The Trois-Frères figure has a name; it's called the "Sorcerer." The Sorcerer is a man (he's not ithyphallic, but he's definitely phallic) hunching forward as if to assume the posture of a quadruped. He has fingers and toes, not hooves, so he's a man. He also has a tail and horns.[4] He looks toward the observer, and he seems to have a man's eyes, set forward-looking in the face rather than along the side of the head. He also seems to have a beard.

Is this a man wearing a deer skin? Is this a man transforming or who has been transformed into a deer? Are those two different ways of saying the same thing? Is this a god, whose representation shows us that he has some kinship between mankind and deer? Knowing more about the culture of the artist would certainly give us more information to aid in interpretation. Did the artist hunt and eat deer? Was he representing the idea that he and his prey were of the same herd, ruled by the same gods? Was he showing his superiority to his prey, manifested in his ability to deceive the deer into believing he was one of them?

We're only guessing. But any guesses we can conceivably make about these two images put us squarely onto the fantasy shelf in the bookstore. Analogy, magic, the gods, surprise; these are the magician's tools for sneaking up on the right brain to surprise it and shake meaning out of it.

Giorgio de Santillana and Hertha von Dechend famously suggested that mythology was preliterate man's tool for passing down technical astronomical information.[5] That's a hypothesis worth taking seriously, but it can't possibly explain all of mythology. The fact that the Greeks looked into the night sky and saw Perseus, his steed Pegasus, the princess Andromeda to be rescued, King Cepheus (hard to see), and Queen Cassiopeia (very visible), and the threatening sea monster to which the King and Queen were offering their daughter as sacrifice, does not simply mean that that story was a convenient way to remember the layout of the night sky. The ancients did not invent arbitrary stories because those stories helped them navigate, pick the days of their sacred festivals, or calculate the precession of the equinoxes. Something about the stories themselves made the stories leap out of the night sky, and then the stories were also convenient vehicles for holding numerical details corresponding to days in the Synodic Period of Venus or years in the Sothic Cycle. And since the celestial realm was understood to determine events on Earth, that means that the gods and monsters, murders and rescues, sacrifices and sacrileges, all drove meaning and even events in human life.

Tropes of Fantasy

Fantasy contains many subgenres within it, and the tropes in any novel can vary accordingly. Overall, the most common tropes of fantasy literature, especially epic fantasy, are:

- *The Broken World.* The whole world is poisoned by the death of a god, the loss of an ancient covenant, or a grievous sin. As bad as things are now, they are going to get worse if the rupture is not healed.

- *The Chosen One.* Only one person can fix this situation. Because of bloodline or prophesy or some rightful inheritance, the burden to heal the world falls on one set of shoulders.

- *The Dark Lord.* Behind the great wound in the cosmos stands a fallen angel, a wizard driven mad, or wounded god. It is his rage or cold desire for power or vengeance that oppresses and threatens the world.

- *The Mentor.* Our protagonist is given key initial information to get him on his path by an older hero, a wizard or a warrior with wisdom and skills but who himself doesn't have the power to defeat the Dark Lord. The Mentor looks very powerful to the hero at first, but that won't last. Not only must the Chosen One surpass the Mentor, but the Mentor will die or be removed from the quest before the hero feels he can stand on his own two feet.

- *The Damsel in Distress.* The hero's romantic life is tied to his success in his quest. To find requited love, he must become the champion who can defeat the Dark Lord, because this will impress the damsel, free her, or make him worthy of her.

- *The Quest.* The hero's central task lies at the end of a long journey, often a physical journey. Along the way he will face and defeat a series of guardians or overcome a series of obstacles, each greater than the one before, each step demanding from him new insights, growth, or allies.

- *Magic.* The magic of myth and legend is real. There are magical items. The hero may have a unique magical power or be bonded to a magical artifact of unique power. Alternatively, the hero may be a magicless everyman up against forces that are all magically empowered.

We can't even scrape the surface of ancient myth. The point is this; before man could write, he was using the tools of fantasy literature. When he shows up with the first written stories—Perseus, but also Gilgamesh and the Pandavas and Susanoo—he is still using them.

Let's fast forward to the Middle Ages.

Tropes of Science Fiction

Science fiction similarly contains within a wide range of types of stories. Still, here are six extremely common science fiction tropes:

- *The Scientist Hero.* Characteristically, the hero of science fiction is a thinker. He might not literally be a scientist and he might still be a man of action, but he will win by using his brain—and possibly a new scientific insight—rather than his heart.
- *The Galactic Empire.* Representative democracy didn't work out for some reason. The future is always built of an empire or competing empires.
- *Handwavium.* Science has advanced so far that mankind has tools that might as well be magic. How do they work? We get no explanation, a high-level explanation, or complete babble—a waving of the magician's hands.
- *Artificial Intelligence.* In the future, our tools not only appear to us to be aware, they are in fact aware.
- *Mysterious Ancient Civilizations.* We were not the first civilization to inhabit this place. Strange ruins lie in the empty places, containing long-forgotten demons but also great insights, waiting for us to harvest them.
- *Optimism.* Mankind can conquer. We are not limited by constraints of resources, time, or energy. Vision can be accomplished.

King Arthur Meets the Printing Press:
Thomas Malory's *Le Morte d'Arthur*

Thomas Malory didn't invent King Arthur. It's not clear whether King Arthur was in fact invented as opposed to being a man who actually lived, or a British god who was imagined into mortal form to disguise him from Christian censors, or something else entirely. In any case, he's an old story, the great myth of Britain. Arthur appeared in many literary sources before Malory got hold of him, including the *Book of Taliesin* (which contains a poem, the *Spoils of Annwfn*, recounting a journey by Arthur to another world), Nennius's *Historia Brittonum* (which describes Arthur as an explicitly Christian war leader but not as a king, and identifies twelve great battles of Arthur), Geoffrey of Monmouth's *Historia Regum Britanniae* (Geoffrey makes Arthur king of Britain and married to Guinevere and also introduces Merlin as a prophet and wizard), and Wolfram von Eschenbach's *Parzival* (which contained the quest for the holy grail).

Thomas Malory himself was a knight, a member of Parliament, and in and out of prison for political reasons as well as for committing actual crimes during the Wars of the Roses. These crimes included violent robbery, horse theft, and rape.[6] The jarring inconsistency of a violent thug writing a great work about knightly ideals has led some scholars to try to find a different Thomas Malory to whom to attribute authorship of *Le Morte d'Arthur*, but no one with any alternate theory has managed to persuade other scholars. It seems that we must live with the likelihood that a violent brute wrote the great epic of chivalry. The author himself does tell us that he's writing the book in prison, after all. We just need to have a clear and unromantic understanding of the reasons why a man might be in prison in the fifteenth century.

Le Morte itself compiles stories from numerous other sources, legendary and poetic. Malory didn't invent Arthur, then, and he didn't even invent the stories he was telling about Arthur. What was his accomplishment?

Two things are interesting about what Malory achieved. First, he told the story of Arthur from start to finish, focusing principally on Arthur. That is to say, he didn't insert some information about Arthur into a larger history, and he didn't write a poem recounting a single Arthurian deed, he told the entire story of Arthur.

And second, he was published by William Caxton. Malory is thought to have completed his work in 1470, so manuscript copies of the book may have circulated (there is a "Winchester Manuscript" that contains a version of *Le Morte d'Arthur* apparently written in the 1470s that is different from the printed texts). In 1485, William Caxton published *Le Morte d'Arthur*.[7]

★ ★ ★
Rosicrucian Fantasy

Another quirky pre-modern fantasy is to be found in the three seventeenth-century documents published about (and perhaps by?) the Rosicrucians (who may not have existed), the *Fama Fraternitatis*, the *Confessio Fraternitatis*, and especially *The Chymical Wedding of Christian Rosencreutz*. The last, especially, has been described by historian Frances Yates as an "alchemical fantasia"—it is a chivalric allegory *cum* ascent text in which the title character is initiated over seven days, in a castle full of mechanical and alchemical wonders, into an elite spiritual knighthood.

Caxton was an Englishman who spent many years in Belgium. While there he founded a printing press which he used to print his own translation of a collection of stories relating to the *Iliad*. When he returned to England, the demand for his own book was strong enough that he established a printing press in England, believed to be the first in the country. He published his own work, Chaucer, various other things, and *Le Morte d'Arthur*.[8]

So in Arthuriana, Thomas Malory was in the right place at the right time. Others wrote about Arthur before him and after, but he wrote a book about Arthur right as the printing press hit Arthur's homeland, and his book hit it big. Like J. K. Rowling publishing just in time to have her work promoted by the new tool of e-commerce, the new technology of printing made Malory dominant.

Other than as a neat historical note about publishing and a parable about the effects of technology, why have I included Malory's work? Because in *Le Morte d'Arthur*, we finally get the full-blown Arthur, recognizable as the Arthur we know, who is the hero of an epic fantasy. Merlin? Check. Nimue? Check. Utopian Camelot that cannot last in this fallen world? Check. Here we have the round table, the sword Excalibur given by the Lady of the Lake, and the grail quest. We also have Arthur's grave sin, his begetting of his son Mordred by incest, which leads to Mordred's revealing the adultery of Guinevere and Lancelot so that Lancelot is exiled. Without its great defender, Camelot falls apart. Arthur kills Mordred but Mordred kills Arthur as well, and Bedivere throws Excalibur back to the Lady in the Lake.

And perhaps in Camelot's end we should see the resolution of the conflict between the apparently brutal life of Thomas Malory and his authorship of the epic. Camelot cannot survive contact with sinful mankind. The great knight Lancelot sins, and so does the great king Arthur. Their sins give the lie to their chivalric oaths and destroy the knightly paradise that could have been. What man could write this conclusion more honestly than a knight and Member of Parliament who was also a robber and a rapist?

The Travels of Sir John Mandeville

The Middle Ages produced some classics of travel literature, including *A Masterpiece to Those Who Contemplate the Wonders of Cities and the Marvels of Traveling* by Ibn Battuta and the *Travels of Benjamin of Tudela*. These books both contain interesting historical information about Muslim, Jewish, and Christian communities around the Mediterranean in the Middle Ages and are fairly sober accounts.

The Travels of Sir John Mandeville, by contrast, are wild. The tamer elements include the account of a Christian king named Prester John in a city called Nisa on the island of Pentoxoire from which Prester John ruled the seventy-two isles of India (allotopian literature raises its head again). This has a biblical feel, with the seventy-two isles corresponding to the seventy-two nations of the Earth,[9] and the *Travels* also report Bible-related legends, like the grains of paradise growing the wood of the cross. But the *Travels* also blandly assert the existence of Cyclopes, men with heads sunken into their chests, and the dying and rising phoenix bird.

There's no evidence that there ever was a John Mandeville.[10] He seems to be a complete invention, and this book was stitched together in his name. By "stitched together," I mean that large chunks of the *Travels* are known to be taken from pre-existing travel narratives. So whoever put together the *Travels* had not himself been to any of these places, and is reading travel narratives (or what appear to be travel narratives) at second hand or even more remotely.

But why would an English reading public believe these accounts? Does the provenance of the book—English, clinging to the foggy edge of the known world—have something to do with it? Did the English believe in men without heads because the entire world beyond their smallish island seemed to be awash in the mysterious powers of chaos? Does that have something to do with the persistence

★ ★ ★
Epic

Properly speaking, an epic is a long narrative poem originally composed orally and rooted in *volkswanderung*, the great migration of a people. *The Iliad* is an epic, and so is the *Mahabharata*. *The Odyssey* is not. *The Aeneid* is a fake epic. *The Lord of the Rings* and *The Wheel of Time* are not epics at all (and Tolkien never used the term). Epic literature is certainly one of the roots of fantasy, and we can charitably think that the continued use of the term "epic fantasy" is a way to remember that connection.

of fantasy in modern times as a phenomenon of English literature? Or did the English in fact take the Travels as fiction? Did they enjoy the stories of the fabulous allotopian kingdom of Prester John in the Indies and the death and rebirth of the phoenix as stories, as, in effect, a fantasy novel?

Elizabethan Court Magic:
Edmund Spenser's *The Fairie Queene*

Civil servant Edmund Spenser presented the first three books of his epic poem *The Faerie Queene* to Queen Elizabeth I, clearly hoping to gain royal favor. She duly granted him a life pension, possibly without ever reading the poem. When Spenser died in 1599, he had completed six books of the massive work, as well as fragments of what were probably intended to be the seventh book.[11]

The Faerie Queene uses the devices of fantasy literature. Magic and monsters abound,[12] as do damsels in distress and capricious gods. Here again, the principal character is King Arthur, but Spenser's Arthur is not Malory's Arthur. Across six poetic books, each centered on and allegorizing a different virtue,[13] rides Arthur the knight wildly in love with the titular Faerie Queene. He himself is the virtue Magnificence, the pinnacle and sum of all virtue. Spenser's Arthur is not a tragic man whose sins drag him down to failure, relegating his ideals to a utopian future. *The Fairie Queene* thus makes an implicit rebuttal to *Le Morte d'Arthur*, or perhaps a claim that the ideals of Arthur that could not be realized in the savage violence of the Wars of the Roses now adorned, or could adorn, the court of Elizabeth I—who was obviously the real Faerie Queene.

The Gothic Novel: Horace Walpole's *The Castle of Otranto*

Horace (Horatio) Walpole, the Earl of Orford, was a Whig politician and son of a Whig politician (his father Robert was the first British Prime

Minister). He held government sinecures at the gift of his father, he was a Member of Parliament for two different constituencies, he associated with the feminist-intellectual Blue Stockings Society.[14] Walpole was an interesting person, but his real fame rests on the invention of the Gothic novel.

Some descriptors get attached to novels in such a way that they sound like genres, but in fact they are really aesthetics. This is arguably true of steampunk (see p. 97). It is also true of the "gothic" novel. A gothic novel is one in which reminders of the past are everywhere and a general feeling of fear and uneasiness prevails. Ruins are a common motif, especially the ruins of monumental buildings like castles and churches. Lurid crimes are a common plot device. The gothic novel influenced such writers as Brontë, Dickens, Poe, and Hawthorne. It also touched speculative fiction specifically in Bram Stoker's *Dracula*, Mary Shelley's *Frankenstein*, Robert Louis Stevenson's *Strange Case of Dr. Jekyll and Mr. Hyde*, and Mervyn Peake's *Gormenghast* trilogy (especially the first two books; the third one, weirdly, gets a little steampunk).

And the first gothic novel was Walpole's *The Castle of Otranto*. The novel set the mold for all that was to follow, featuring ghosts, prophecies, a death by stabbing in a church, a prince in disguise, a prisoner in a tower, and various other gothic trappings. Walpole claimed he was inspired to write the novel by a nightmare in which a ghost featured prominently.[15] To the book's second edition Walpole applied the subtitle "A Gothic Story," thus naming the genre he had invented.

The Castle of Otranto is claimed to be the first supernatural English novel. If this is true (you have to disqualify Edmund Spenser and Sir John Mandeville to reach this conclusion, but that seems fair enough), that alone makes the novel noteworthy in a guide to fantasy literature. The fact that the novel also pioneered an aesthetic that has been influential all the way from *The Scarlet Letter* to *Castle Ravenloft* is icing on the gory, ruined cake.

Poet and Visionary: William Blake

William Blake was a visual artist and a poet. He was an engraver and printer, and he put all those skills to work together, illustrating, engraving, and printing his own books of poetry. On top of whatever we might say about the content of his work, we might see him as the patron saint of self-publishing, approximately two hundred years ahead of Jeff Bezos.

William Blake was also a religious visionary. Today when we say "visionary" we usually mean "this CEO has been very good at predicting the patterns of changing consumer demand," but Blake had visions. He saw angels, and God shoving his head into the house through a window, and the demonic spirit of a flea.[16]

In his so-called prophetic books, William Blake anticipated Tolkien by inventing (envisioning?) his own mythology for Britain. The mythology includes four Zoas (who seem to be both divinities and the four parts of the primal man, Albion, before he falls) and four emanations (who seem to be feminine counterparts). So we have a creation myth that feels sort of like the Egyptian Hermopolitan cosmology (with four male-female pairs) but also echoes in Eden. There are other spirits, and the pantheon interacts in a series of poems in which the pantheon does not appear to be completely consistent. This is in fact how an organic mythology, such as the Greek or Indian pantheons, works. A god who appears in one poem, story, or myth to place a particular role may play a different role in a different work, with a different deity taking the original role. In an ancient mythology, this is because different authors created the different works, drawing gods and heroes from the shared mythology to express what was wanted in the work. In Blake's mythology, this is because Blake was a genius.

So on top of the patron saint of self-publishing, we should see Blake as the patron saint of fantasy world-building. He created (saw?) gods and goddesses for his native land, and like the gods and goddesses of the ancient world, he made (perceived?) them as contradictory and inconsistent.

But the Little Mermaid Dies: Hans Christian Andersen

Hans Christian Andersen wrote novels and plays and other works, but what he's overwhelmingly remembered for is his one hundred fifty-six literary fairytales. He wrote for children despite the fact that he never married or had children of his own, and there is good evidence to suggest that Andersen was attracted to men, though it's unclear whether he ever had a homosexual romantic relationship.[17]

Andersen's stories for children draw heavily on the vocabulary out of which fantasy would come—queens, emperors, elves, goblins, the phoenix, and mermaids come immediately to mind. These stories have explicit moralistic points, some of which get lost in the common translation into popular culture. In Andersen's "The Little Mermaid," for instance, the transformed mermaid's feet bleed terribly, and she feels as if she is walking on sharp knives. The prince does not fall in love with her, but she nevertheless rejects the offer to return to her former state by killing the prince and drowns herself instead. This choice to die instead of kill transforms her into a spirit of the air who will eventually go to Heaven.

The Disney adaptation had snappier music, but obliterated what might have seemed to Andersen like the point: that Heaven was to be achieved by self-denial, and maybe specifically by the renunciation of one's forbidden sexual desires.

The Phantasist: George MacDonald

George MacDonald was a Congregationalist minister, but he had only mixed success at the pulpit.[18] As a fantasy novelist and mentor to other fantasy novelists, however, he achieved a certain amount of fame and a great deal of influence. His first fantasy novel (he called it in its subtitle "A Faerie Romance for Men and Women") was *Phantastes*, a dreamlike stream-of-consciousness narrative in which the novel's protagonist, Anodos ("Roadless" in Greek), is transported the day after his twenty-first birthday to Fairy Land. That transit marks this not only as a fantasy story, but as a kind of story called a "portal fantasy," in which the main character has his fantasy adventure in another world (see also, e.g., C. S. Lewis's Narnia tales).

In Fairy Land, Anodos pursues images of female beauty and is hunted by his own shadow. He encounters kobolds, giants, and other monsters. He encounters living marble statues on a sinking island. He becomes a squire to the king Sir Percivale, and they put down an evil cult, but in doing so, Anodos is killed by the monster the cult worships. He awakens on Earth, only twenty-one days having passed.

MacDonald's story shows us the essential spirituality of fantasy literature. The dream-like narrative and images also show us how close fantasy literature is to depth psychology, with its archetypes vomited up from the depths of the unconscious mind. Magic and monsters and the unseen depths of the right brain and the true self are all only two steps from God at most. And because MacDonald went on to mentor other writers—including Lewis Carroll and C. S. Lewis (who made MacDonald a character in his book *The Great Divorce*)—we see in him the social side of the dialog of fantasy literature. Often, the writers know each other.

Socialism's Epic Poet: William Morris

William Morris was not a Christian preacher. He owned a successful decorative arts firm that influence what we would call interior design in Victorian England. He was a socialist who founded the Socialist League in 1884 and then broke with it in 1890. He was also a publisher, founding and running Kelmscott Press. As a writer, he was most famous in his lifetime for his poetry.[19]

Morris wrote science fiction, or at least allotopian fiction. His *News from Nowhere* presented a socialist utopia in a sort of time-traveling portal fantasy reminiscent of Rip Van Winkle—the main character falls asleep and wakes up in an earthly heaven many years later. Not only does this utopia feature common ownership of the means of production, it also lacks marriage and divorce, courts, prisons, and crime. This all was successful, Morris argued, because people liked to work. Whether that's a reasonable assessment of human nature or not, I'll let you judge, but it's the argument Morris is making.

Morris also wrote fantasy, so we see in him maybe the first example of the true ambigenrous (I've just made this word up) SFF writer. His fantasy novel *The Well at the World's End*, originally published by his own Kelmscott Press, has been reprinted repeatedly. Four princes, bored of life in the palace (this is how the story of the Buddha starts), set out to explore the world. We follow the adventures of Ralph, who through various encounters is directed to the well at the world's end. On the way he meets and falls in love with Ursula. They have various adventures, come to the well and drink its waters, which give them life. When they return to Ralph's home, his family castle has been taken by enemies. He frees the castle and restores his parents, who seat him and Ursula as the new king and queen. Interestingly, the novel may have influenced Tolkien, as it features both a king named Gandolf (although the name Gandálfr, appearing in the Völuspá, seems the more likely direct influence) and also a horse named Silverfax.

I'm tempted to say that *The Well at the World's End* shows us that even socialists feel in their heart that there's something intuitively attractive about monarchy. There, I've said it. I think it also shows us that the symbols of fantasy literature, built as they are right into our unconscious mind, are intuitively attractive.

Chess and Pistol Champion: Lord Dunsany

Edward John Moreton Drax Plunkett, generally known in SFF circles as Lord Dunsany (he was the eighteenth baron), was a cousin once removed of Sir Richard Francis Burton, explorer and writer, and may have been cut a little from the same cloth. He was tall and dashing. He was a champion pistoleer and chess player. He fought in the Second Boer War, was wounded in the Easter Uprising, and was in the Irish Army Reserve and British Home Guard during World War Two.[20] And he was hugely influential in fantasy literature.

His first book was *The Gods of Pegāna*, which he paid to publish in 1905, in an arrangement that today we would describe as a vanity press. This is a collection of short stories about Dunsany's invented gods in his invented fantasy world. No stories in his world had been previously published. It was as if—consider this—it was as if Tolkien had published *The Silmarillion* first, before anyone had experienced Middle Earth through the lens of *The Hobbit* and *The Lord of the Rings*. Dunsany paid to publish it himself and went to market with his *Silmarillion*. The reviews were good, and also baffled.

And the book turned a profit, and he never had to pay to publish again.

He wrote more stories set in Pegāna, but Dunsany's most famous fantasy novel (and most famous work) was *The King of Elfland's Daughter*, published in 1924. When parliament tells the lord of Erl that his people wish to be ruled by the King of Elfland, the lord sends his son to Elfland to woo the King's daughter. They are married and have a son, Orion, but she struggles to live easily in Erl, and then misses her child and son when she returns to Elfland. Ultimately, Elfland absorbs Erl, reuniting the couple and satisfying the people of Erl. Throughout the story, Dunsany plays with traditional ideas about the difference between time in the mortal world and time in Elfland as well as folktale motifs about the discomfort of a fairy wife. The book was not especially well received upon publication, but its reputation has grown over time, and it has come to be regarded as one of the classics of the genre.

Not in Kansas Anymore: L. Frank Baum

L. Frank Baum failed in theater and as a newspaper publisher before he wrote his first Oz novel in 1900. He was still working as a reporter when he achieved success as a novelist. Late in life, he also shook a leg trying to get a film studio off the ground.[21] His entrepreneurialism and his willingness to migrate (from New York to South Dakota to Chicago to California) suggest that in the first novel, *The Wonderful Wizard of Oz*, Baum was not Dorothy—he was the wizard.

It's sometimes suggested that swords, castles, and plate armor are stereotypical or even essential trappings of fantasy literature. I'll concede that those images are common, but right there in the early days of twentieth century fantasy literature, we have Baum, the Americanizer. For every castle, Oz has a hot air balloon. For every talking tree, an alderman. For every witch, a leg-shaking entrepreneur and P. T. Barnum-like showman.

King Arthur Gets a Makeover: T. H. White

T. H. White was an Englishman born in Bombay, which may have given him a particular perspective on empire (and perhaps was part of the reason why he sat out World War II as a conscientious objector in Northern Ireland). As a university student at Cambridge, he wrote a thesis on *Le Morte d'Arthur*. He taught for several years and then became a novelist.[22] His science fiction novels and fantasy stories have basically been forgotten, except for a series of Arthurian stories, beginning with *The Sword in the Stone*. *The Sword in the Stone* later became an animated Disney film. The other three parts were *The Queen of Air and Darkness*, *The Ill-Made*

Knight, and *The Candle in the Wind*. All the Arthurian stories were packaged together (with some revision) and released in 1958 as *The Once and Future King*, and a final Arthurian story, *The Book of Merlyn*, came out in 1977, after White's death.

White's Arthur is a very modern Arthur. (As a bonus, White is not only charming, but very funny.) The conceit that brings about Arthur as anachronism is delightful; Merlyn lives backward in time, so he is fully familiar with the concepts of the future, social and technological. He teaches young Arthur to be a deliberately futuristic king (in White's view), interested in learning and rule by consensus, the great ongoing theme being that Arthur, the round table, and Camelot seek to establish the primacy of right over might. It's difficult not to see in this White's own opposition to Britain's participation in World War II. There may be some chronological chauvinism in this version of Arthur, White assuming that if only medieval monarchs had his ideals, their people could have had better lives. It's a common enough belief among human beings that our generation is the pinnacle of evolution and progress. It will be up to some future writer of Arthuriana to take White on in the mythos.

Chapter Two

EARLY SCIENCE FICTION

The roots of science fiction in some sense must be as deep as the roots of science. The mythologists who embedded numerical sequences into the story of Samson in the Book of Judges or in the tale of Amlethus as recorded by Saxo Grammaticus[1] were scientists and they lived a long time ago. But stories raising what-if questions about human technology began relatively late.

And they involved a surprising number of trips to the moon.

SFF: An Anglo-American Genre?

A quick scan down the table of contents will tell you that most of the writers I touch on in this book wrote in the English language. The major obvious exception, Jules Verne, denied that what he wrote was science fiction (see p. 23, and by the way, Cyrano de Bergerac would have denied it as well, or at least he would have had no idea what you were asking him). Until recently, science fiction and fantasy literature were principally a product of the English language.

There were always honorable exceptions, of course, mostly not covered in this book. For instance, Stanislaw Lem was a prolific Polish writer, many of whose works were science fiction, most famously including the novel *Solaris*, which is about human astronauts trying and failing to communicate with an extraterrestrial intelligence (if you watched the 2002 George Clooney film adaption (the third time *Solaris* was filmed, by the way), and you didn't catch that the likely inability of humankind to communicate with a truly alien intelligence was the story's theme ... you weren't alone). More recently, Chinese writers have made a splash, most notably Liu Cixin, whose *Remembrance of Earth's Past* series, a hard science fiction epic exploring first contact with a hostile alien force, has been adapted both as a Chinese film and as a Netflix series.

Still, the center of gravity of speculative fiction seems to be the English language. Why that might be the case is an interesting question. Someone should write a story about that.

A Classical Moon Voyage: Lucian of Samosata

Lucian of Samosata was a sarcastic son of a bitch. This makes it difficult to know much about him, because all we have to go by is his own writings, which are thoroughly sarcastic, tongue-in-cheek, and satirical. What we think we know is that he was a second-century AD Hellenized (i.e., Greek-speaking and incorporated into the common Greek civilization of the Mediterranean at the time) Syrian. His native language was probably Syriac, which is a form of Aramaic. Then we have a bunch of educational details that may or may not be fictional regarding his family, failing to become a sculptor, running away to get an education, and so on. He may have been a university lecturer for a while, he may have lived in Athens, he may have ended his career as an official of the Egyptian government.[2]

But Lucian probably never went to the moon. Nevertheless, in his book *A True Story*, in a first-person narrative, he recounted a journey to the moon. He gets there by accident via a whirlwind (shades of Oz). There he gets embroiled in a conflict between the sun and the moon (inhabited by non-humans whom Lucian describes) over who should rule Venus. The sun wins by withholding its light and then the parties reach a peace accord.

It's worth noting that the book continues with Lucian returning to Earth, where he encounters, among other things, a sea of milk and an island of cheese. And there's no real technological aspect to Lucian's story—he travels by whirlwind. So perhaps there's an argument that this story is best described as "fantasy." Still, journeys in space are such a mainstay of science fiction that it's commonplace for commentators to say that this is the first science fiction story ever written.

And hey, given how sarcastic Lucian was and how hard it is to parse the real facts out of what he says, maybe he went to the moon.

More Journeys to the Moon: The Selenites

Apparently, the moon is an alluring target, because other proto-science fiction writers imagined traveling there. Oxford-educated clergyman Francis Godwin received his first clerical living under Queen Elizabeth I and was an Anglican priest until his death. He was a scholar who wrote works with titles like *Catalogue of the Bishops of England since the first planting of the Christian Religion in this Island*.[3] And in 1638, five years after his death, his story *The Man in the Moone, or a Discourse of a Voyage thither, by Domingo Gonsales*, was published. The protagonist is carried to the moon by a bird. In the same year, fellow-Anglican priest John Wilkins, who during his career very unusually headed a college at both Oxford and Cambridge, published his treatise *The Discovery of a World in the Moone*. Whereas Godwin's publication was fiction, Wilkins's was a scientific treatise arguing that the moon might indeed be home to living beings, whom he called "Selenites." Wilkins certainly knew Godwin's work, including his moon story, so in the seventeenth century we have an example of science fiction directing science.

In a direction that was ultimately falsified.

Cyrano de Bergerac (or at least a cartoon version of him) has been immortalized in film by Gerard Depardieu as well as, indirectly, Steve

Martin.[4] He lived fast and died young in the first half of the seventeenth century. He was a playwright and a duelist, and he also wrote novels, including his *Comical History of the States and Empires of the Moon*.[5] In this novel, his protagonist, named Cyrano, launches himself to the moon with a rocket belt, so we finally have an unambiguous technological what-if as well as a voyage through space. The inhabitants of the moon are favorably impressed by Cyrano's nose, a self-deprecating detail that is irresistibly charming. He meets Domingo Gonsales, Francis Godwin's protagonist, so Cyrano's tale is directly intertextual, setting itself up as a sequel and answer to the other man's book!

Daniel Defoe was a man of many careers, including spy, in the late seventeenth and early eighteenth centuries.[6] As a writer, he is much more famous for *Robinson Crusoe*, *Moll Flanders*, *A Journal of the Plague Year*, etc., but in 1705 he also published *The Consolidator; or, Memoirs of Sundry Transactions from the World in the Moon*. The narrator rides a "chariot" to the moon. This is sometimes described as the first space-ship in fiction, but if so, this spaceship is pulled by feathered, winged creatures, so again we're really on that borderline space between science fiction and fantasy.

Still, a trip to the moon!

Science as Monster: Mary Shelley

Mary Wollstonecraft Shelley née Godwin was raised and educated by her anarchist father. At the age of seventeen, she took up with Percy Bysshe Shelley, one of her father's political compatriots and a married man. Hard years of debt and social isolation followed, as well as the death of her infant daughter, before Shelley's wife committed suicide and they were able to marry.[7]

In the year of that suicide, 1816, the Shelleys famously spent the summer on Lake Geneva with Lord Byron and John Polidori (fun fact: this

Provocateur

My favorite story about Daniel Defoe is when he was sentenced to the stocks for writing a political pamphlet that had enraged the establishment, his friends came along with him . . . and brought copies of the pamphlet to sell.

summer figures heavily into the amazing Tim Powers novel, *The Stress of Her Regard*; see p. 94). During discussions with that literary crew, Mary Shelley conceived the idea that would eventually become her novel *Frankenstein; or, The Modern Prometheus*. She published the novel two years later, at the age of twenty.

Here the term "gothic novel" rears its head again, because *Frankenstein* is definitely a gothic novel, full of murders and premonitions and scientific discovery told as horror. The fact that a fantasy novel can be described as "gothic" and so can a science fiction novel and so can a novel that has neither supernatural nor technological elements is a good indication that "gothic" is an aesthetic, and not a genre.

The monster, famously, is not Frankenstein. Victor Frankenstein is the scientist who creates the monster, who refuses to create a female companion for the monster even as he himself courts a wife, and who is ultimately destroyed by the monster. The monster's name is Adam. But of course, the real question the novel asks is, Is the scientist the monster after all?

Is science, after all, potentially a monster?

The Extraordinary Journeys: Jules Verne

Frenchman Jules Verne was the scion of a well-to-do family whose father wanted him to study law. Like many lawyers and would-be lawyers before and since, he got sidetracked into a literary career. Notably, he did not regard himself as a science fiction writer. When asked, he denied that he wrote science fiction, pointing out that submarines already existed when he wrote about them. Arguably, Verne is better thought of as a travel and adventure writer. His famous novels were all published in partnership with Pierre-Jules Hetzel in a single series called *Voyages extraordinaires*, i.e., *Extraordinary Journeys*.[8] His was a great age of travel and the stories are all stories of travel. And many of those novels contain nothing resembling science fiction. *Around the World in Eighty Days* takes place on trains and in air balloons and on the backs of elephants. And the extraordinary travel element in *Michael Strogoff* is an epic journey across Russia by sled.[9]

But some of the journeys do have science fictional elements. Submarines had been invented in Verne's time, but they weren't going *Twenty Thousand Leagues under the Sea* like Nemo's *Nautilus* did. The *Journey to the Center of the Earth* in Verne's book didn't happen in a big machine, but it was a lost-world journey worthy of H. Rider Haggard or Edgar Rice Burroughs. And of course, Verne wrote not one but two books, *From the Earth to the Moon* and *Around the Moon*, about the Baltimore Gun Club firing people to the moon in a "Columbiad space gun." Verne's moon sadly, but accurately, turns out to be barren and void of inhabitants.

So if his sending characters to the moon allows us to count Lucian of Samosata as an early science fiction writer, I think we have to admit Verne. But I also think that if anyone suggests that he was the "father of science fiction" or anything similar, it's appropriate for us to raise a modest objection or two.

Editors, Amirite?

Hetzel apparently rewrote much of Verne and did the same to Balzac. Many of Verne's later novels were rewritten by Verne's son Michel.

The Socialist Sociologist: H. G. Wells

H. G. Wells was the youngest son of an irregularly-employed cricket player and a domestic servant. He overcame a turbulent family situation, an irregular education, and an unhappy apprenticeship by virtue of his skill at Latin, eventually winning a scholarship to the Normal School of Science in London, where he studied biology. While there, he became interested in the Fabian Society and attended lectures at the home of William Morris (see p. 14). After graduation, to supplement his income, he began writing, initially publishing humorous articles.[10] In 1895, he published his first novel, *The Time Machine*.

With H. G. Wells, we seem to finally get to a writer who was writing science fiction and knew it. Maybe it's because he had university training in science. Maybe it's because his first novel was obviously science fiction, not just in the conceit, time travel, but also in the mechanism, which was technological, and in the narrative, which is a kind of a dystopia. In any case, his "scientific romances" included *The Invisible Man*, *The War of the Worlds*, *The Island of Dr. Moreau*, *The Shape of Things to Come*, and *The First Men in the Moon* (oops, there's that moon again; Wells's protagonists get to the moon by using an antigravitic element called "cavorite" and find insectoid inhabitants they call, unoriginally, "Selenites").

Wells was a socialist who longed for and articulated a socialist future. His *The Shape of Things to Come*, published in 1933, was remarkable for predicting a Second World War that would break out initially between Germany and Poland. He's also due credit for some prescience in foreseeing the aerial bombardment of whole cities. On the other hand, Wells also imagined Spain and the UK staying out of the war and Poland fighting Hitler to a draw, so his foresight was limited.

We can debate whether or not he missed the mark in describing how the conflict would end. He recounts a "Dictatorship of the Air" coming from those who control the world's surviving means of transportation. This dictatorship promotes science and English and bans religion and eventually brings the world to utopia. Obviously, this didn't happen . . . except that if you said "managerial class" or "Machiavellians" rather than "Dictatorship of the Air," you'd sound a lot like James Burnham.

So what happens next, after the dictatorship of the managerial class . . . er, the air? In the novel, the dictatorship fades when it is no longer needed, leaving a classless society dedicated to the pursuit of knowledge.

Now how likely does that seem?

Thinking Machines: Samuel Butler

Samuel Butler was educated at Cambridge to enter the Anglican clergy, winning there a first in Classics in 1858. On the eve of ordination, he had second thoughts and emigrated to New Zealand (this was a dramatic move in the nineteenth century). He lived there for five years herding sheep before selling his farm and flocks to return to London.[11] In 1863 he published a letter in *The Press*, a New Zealand newspaper, signing it "Cellarius." The letter was a response to *On the Origin of Species*, and was entitled "Darwin among the Machines." In the letter, Butler predicted that machines would come to evolve more quickly than humans, eventually replacing us.

Returning to England, Butler spent the next eight years finishing his masterpiece, *Erewhon; or, Over the Range.* ("Erewhon" is "nowhere" backward.) It was initially published anonymously, but received general admiration and he eventually came forward as the author. Then he spent the rest of his life as a retired gentleman of means, his only other significant publication being a posthumous semi-autobiographical novel, *The Way of All Flesh.*

Erewhon is an allotopia, not clearly either a utopia or a dystopia. In it, Butler continues to explore the theme of machine evolution and also develops the idea of artificial intelligence. This is the first novel in which machines are not only conscious, but dangerous, so that Erewhonians choose to protect themselves by living deliberately without machines.

Now that surely sounds crazy.

Froggie Went a-Courtin' on Mars: Edgar Rice Burroughs

Edgar Rice Burroughs was an American. After early discharge from the US Cavalry due to a heart problem, he knocked around doing various jobs, including cowboying, managing a mine, and wholesaling pencil sharpeners. He got into writing novels because he was convinced he could do it, and he needed to make money. To avoid the public shame of being a pulp novelist, he initially published under the name Norman Bean.[12]

You have to admire Burroughs's prolific output. You also have to admire his business acumen; the guy exploited his "IPs," as we would say now, like no one ever had, developing comic strips and movies (*Tarzan of the Apes* was released in 1918) as well as various novelties. Some of his writing, especially in long-running or knockoff series, became tedious or repetitive. But some of his novels are genuine classics.

One of those is *A Princess of Mars*, one of the great planetary romances. Originally serialized in 1912 as *Under the Moons of Mars*, this story again features space travel by a mystical rather than a technological means. Protagonist John Carter goes to sleep on Earth and wakes up on Mars. Once we're on Mars ("Barsoom" to the locals), though, we get trappings that would eventually become classics in science fiction, such as airships (traveling using the "eighth Barsoomian ray") and lightning weapons (Barsoom's technologies are decidedly pseudoscientific, as are those of, say, *Star Wars*). The native races use firearms that fire exploding shells. But Carter principally fights with his cavalryman's sword and the strength advantage that being on a lower-gravity planet gives him. And, of course, with his chivalrous and generous character.

Chapter Three

PULP-PLUS

When the SFF scene opened, a generation or more of the writers of science fiction and fantasy rose out of the pulp magazines (see the sidebar on p. 75). Here are some of the greatest of them.

More than Just Conan: Robert E. Howard

Robert E. Howard lived in Texas all his life. At the age of nine, he started writing his own stories, imitating his heroes Jack London and Rudyard Kipling. He worked odd jobs and at the age of eighteen he got his first professional sale, a caveman story that was published in *Weird Tales*. With this sale, he dropped out of the stenography course he had enrolled in and set out to write full time.

Like many writers, he struggled financially and continued to take odd jobs, writing oil news, delivering mail, and working as a soda jerk. Over the next twelve years, he published in various magazines, all of them pulps. His mother contracted tuberculosis and entered a long slow decline in health. Howard developed several iconic characters, the two most famous being the Puritan avenger Solomon Kane and Conan the Cimmerian. He began a long correspondence with H. P. Lovecraft (see below), who called him "Two-Gun Bob." His earnings steadily rose, exceeding $2,000 in 1935, and in 1936, when he was thirty years old, he was at a peak in popularity.

And that year, on the day when he learned that his mother had entered a coma from which she was not expected to awaken, he got into his car and shot himself in the head.[1]

Some writers will sneer at Howard as a pulp writer, but really that is just a designation for the venues where he published. There's a lot to say about and for Robert E. Howard. He had distinctive ideas that came through in his fiction, including the notion of ancestral memories, and the conceit that civilization was inherently decadent, and from time to time required renewal in the form of overrunning barbarian hordes. In his writing, he respected masculine virtues of physical courage and honor. His heroes minced no words and gave not an inch. He created not one but two characters who were so iconic that they made it to the big screen multiple times and inspired other writers to take up the pen and write stories featuring them. He died young, giving every indication that he would have gone on to even greater fame, influence, and financial success.

And he was also a great writer. He wrote spare, muscular prose and lyrical poetry as well. If you've never read Howard and are surprised to hear the writing of the Conan the Barbarian guy praised, I advise you to start with the Conan novella *Beyond the Black River.*

You might well find that you keep going.

The Spirit of the Storm

"Not all men seek rest and peace; some are born with the spirit of the storm in their blood, restless harbingers of violence and bloodshed, knowing no other path."
—Robert E. Howard

Eldritch Horrors, Foreigners, and Fish: H. P. Lovecraft

Howard's peer and correspondent H. P. Lovecraft also lived a tragically short life, dying of intestinal cancer at the age of forty-six, his poverty likely being a factor in his death. Lovecraft wasn't born poor, but his family's wealth dissipated after the death of his grandfather and both his parents were institutionalized. The decline and rot in old families and madness are both recurring themes in Lovecraft's writing. New England, where he spent most of his life, is the persistent setting. Lovecraft wrote what he knew, and what he feared.[2]

On the surface, what he seemed to fear most was foreigners and fish. I'm not one to rush to condemn writers of the past for not sharing my views on race (or anything else, really), but Lovecraft did indeed seem to distrust and fear foreigners and anyone swarthy, featuring them often as cultists worshipping implacable hostile gods, eating away at the fringes of the declining Western civilization. And many of those implacable hostile gods bore more than a passing resemblance to aquatic life. Dagon was a humanoid fish (and indeed is based on the Canaanite Dagon, whose name means something like the Fish One). Cthulhu had a head like an octopus. And the Deep Ones are fish-like humanoids who mate with human beings, producing disturbing (and vaguely foreign-looking) hybrids.

But there's something more interesting than that going on with Lovecraft. The other thing he seemed to fear—and believe devoutly in—was a meaningless existence. The cosmic demons of the "Cthulhu Mythos" (a term coined by another writer) don't hate humanity. They don't care about humanity. They may not even notice humanity's existence at all. Humanity are bugs, bacteria, nothing. That realization is the horrific epiphany that drives the best of Lovecraft's stories—that after all, we are nothing but meaningless meat.

Lovecraft published in the pulps, most prominently in *Weird Tales*. Despite publishing reasonably prolifically, he was never able to support himself financially. His wife left him, and he died alone, in poverty and obscurity.

But then a strange thing happened. Like a zombie, his own career rose from the grave. This happened first of all because of other writers. Lovecraft was a reasonably prolific writer of fiction, but he was a hugely prolific correspondent, and he maintained long-distance relationships with many writers. These writers championed him during his life and continued to champion him after his death, pushing to keep his work in print and to write new stories featuring the alien demons of the mythos he had created, also expanding the mythos. August Derleth founded Arkham House in part to keep Lovecraft's works in print (Arkham is a fictional Massachusetts town created by Lovecraft for his stories), and then Arkham House became a platform to launch the careers of other writers.[3]

In the 1970s, scholars took up the study of Lovecraft. And then gamers did, first and most famously Sandy Peterson, who turned this bleak universe of horror stories into a tabletop roleplaying game called *Call of Cthulhu*. This game, now in its seventh edition, has been a perennial TTRPG favorite since, the classic horror roleplaying game, and in October 2024 it became the second inductee into the ENNIES Hall of Fame (after Dungeons & Dragons).[4] *Call of Cthulhu* then spawned waves of other games implementing Lovecraft's themes and characters in boardgame, card game, and videogame formats. Lovecraftian movies have been made. Writers up and down the spectrum of fame have acknowledged Lovecraft as an influence. From 1975 through 2015, the World Fantasy Award trophy was a caricature bust of H. P. Lovecraft, affectionately referred to as the "Howie." Whatever Lovecraft himself had in mind when he was mentoring and corresponding with those other writers, that turned out be an effective strategy for a stellar post-mortem career.

Our recent wave of disdaining dead people for not sharing our political views has hit Lovecraft. It seems to me as of this writing that the academics, writers, and others he has influenced are a large and devoted enough cadre that Lovecraft's reputation has—mostly—survived (the Howie is the big obvious casualty, having been replaced by a statuette of a tree in front of a full moon). Yes, we can acknowledge, Lovecraft believed things that would be impolite to say in any drawing room today (and would have been impolite in many drawing rooms in the 1930s). Nevertheless, he introduced us to a different kind of horror, one that has stayed with us.

Fandom and Fandoms

Here's a key that you do not need to have to enjoy SFF literature, but that helps explain some of its features as well as the ferocity of some of its struggles. Historically, a large number of the writers, visual artists, editors, publishers, reviewers, and even readers of science fiction and fantasy have known each other. The context in which these people have interacted is often called "fandom," a word that, confusingly, can mean other things. Let's clarify.

"Fandom" can mean the social group of people that produces and reads SFF literature. It means this mostly in historical contexts, e.g., when discussing the dynamics of what the Hugo Awards represent and why they erupted into controversy in 2015 (see p. 144). It also has this meaning if you hear it at World Fantasy or maybe certain parts of Dragon Con or especially Worldcon, where the aging survivors of the golden age of fandom still congregate, now with their canes and electric scooters, to repeat their age-old rituals of recognition and celebration.

In other contexts, a "fandom" means enthusiasts for a particular kind of art, or the enthusiasm felt by those fans. In other words, anime art has a fandom—people who like anime. And the answer to the question, "What are your fandoms?" might be "I love anime and cyberpunk and especially *Attack on Titan.*"

By the way, the word "fan" is short for "fanatic" and ultimately derives from the Latin "fanum," meaning a temple or shrine. To be a fan of something is to be religiously devoted to it. I personally don't love to use this word to describe either myself or any of my readers, but I know not everyone is a philologist and this is probably a losing battle. And the truth is, the veneration some of the old-time fans have for their community (and that some anime watches have for *Cowboy Bebop*) does seem to border on worship.

The Psychohistorian: Isaac Asimov

Isaac Asimov immigrated from Russia to the US at the age of three in 1920. He graduated high school at fifteen and got his bachelor's degree at nineteen, publishing his first short stories at the same time.[5]

Asimov wrote a lot. It wasn't all great. I read his one-volume commentary on the Bible in college and found it pretty banal, mostly noteworthy for the fact that, like Samuel Johnson's preaching woman, it existed at all. He went through phases, writing a lot of fiction for years, then non-fiction for years, then fiction again. He was regarded as one of the "Big Three" science fiction writers of his day, with Clarke and Heinlein (see below).

Arguably Asimov's most famous idea is his three laws of robotics, presented as three maxims incorporated into robots as a safety feature:

- The First Law: A robot may not injure a human being or, through inaction, allow a human being to come to harm.
- The Second Law: A robot must obey the orders given it by human beings except where such orders would conflict with the First Law.
- The Third Law: A robot must protect its own existence as long as such protection does not conflict with the First or Second Law.[6]

I think Asimov's most famous series, though, is his *Foundation* books. He published the first stories in what would become the series at the age of twenty-two, and they read like it. The writing is swift, self-confident, and a little green. Still, the stories contained a big idea, an idea big enough that the first short stories were post together and published as a so-called "fix-up novel," and Asimov then wrote sequels.

Asimov's big idea really came from the Book of Isaiah. In Isaiah 10 and 11, the prophet foresees a "remnant" in a future day that will have his prophecies, which will lead them to repent and return to the Jerusalem from which they have been driven. Transposed into the key of science fiction, this is the idea that drives *Foundation* and its sequels. A future galactic empire is crumbling. A scientist whose ability to predict future history by applying laws of mass psychology sees the end coming and prepares for it by launching a group of encyclopedists to the remote corner of the galaxy. From beyond the grave, using a combination of recorded messages and other tricks, he then guides them to survive the thousand-year night after the collapse of the empire, to eventually re-found galactic civilization.

(If you're reading this and thinking with some disappointment that the recent streaming program based on *Foundation* was a travesty that turned this interesting big science fiction idea into a show about a girl with magic powers, you are correct.)

Psychohistorian Hari Seldon is the Prophet Isaiah, guiding the remnant that will return. On a sort of meta or recursive level, Isaac Asimov, presenting this idea as author, is the Prophet Isaiah, preaching to the remnant that will return. Now if we could only find evidence that the Prophet Isaiah in chapters 10 and 11 of his book was really writing about Asimov writing about Seldon, we'd have three lovely little Russian nesting dolls and also an ouroboros biting its tail.

That would have made Asimov's Bible commentary interesting.

The Futurist: Arthur C. Clarke

Arthur C. Clarke, the second of the "Big Three," grew up on an English farm. He published stories in fanzines in his late teens and early twenties. He served in the Royal Air Force during World War II as a radar specialist, had his first professional short story sale in 1946 and published his first novel in 1948. In 1956, Clarke emigrated to Sri Lanka, where he lived until his death.[7]

Clarke (who, by the way, also wrote about space stations, immersive virtual-reality games, tablet computers, voice interfaces with computers, and personalized advertisements, among other things) wrote a famous first-contact story in which mankind encounters, not another species, but another species' artifacts. *Rendezvous with Rama* tells the story of a massive cylinder that passes through our solar system, and how Earth astronauts intercept it, enter it, and explore the strange ecosystem inside.

The book was a thought experiment in interstellar travel technology and the consequences of building spaceships so massive, they might contain their own weather systems.

Hilariously, then, when a massive cylinder from somewhere in deep space actually entered our solar system in 2017, changed course around the Sun, and left again, we did two things. First, we didn't name the object "Rama." We named it "'Oumuamua." What a goof! (Yes, okay, the tradition is that the spotting observatory chooses the label, and the observatory in Hawaii gave the object the name, which means "scout" in Hawaiian, and that *is* a pretty good name to apply to an alien object entering our solar system . . . but still. It should have been "Rama.")[8]

The other thing we did is that we almost missed it. 'Oumuamua only got spotted on its way out, and then we quickly lost track of it, because, as one astronomer explained to me, in technical language, "Space is really big." So we weren't in time to explore the object, and maybe we missed our first contact opportunity.

Or maybe we didn't. The majority position is that 'Oumuamua is probably a nine-hundred-yard-long cylindrical rock (such rocks are very common, of course) that just coincidentally winged in from the immensity of deep space to bend its course around our sun (insert eye-roll emoji here). But the chief proponent of the alternative view, the view that says we ought to take seriously the possibility that we just missed a Rama moment, is Avi Loeb, a theoretical physicist who is also the longest-serving chair of Harvard's Astronomy Department, and not an intellect to sneer at.

But the point is, Arthur C. Clarke was there first, and he helped define how we are talking about this experience we just had. Or almost had.

From Juveniles to Free Love: Robert Heinlein

Robert A. Heinlein served as a radio communications officer in the US Navy until his discharge in 1934 due to pulmonary tuberculosis. In

1939, after years of trying his hand at various occupations as well as progressive politics, he started writing (and selling) science fiction stories. During the war, he worked for the Navy again as a civilian employee, and after the war, he returned to literature.[9]

Heinlein was the first science fiction writer to break into mainstream literary venues, publishing a series of four short stories in *The Saturday Evening Post*. He also wrote a pioneering series of "juveniles," science fiction books for young adult readers featuring teenage boy protagonists, which were published one a year for twelve years ending in 1958. The book which was to be the thirteenth in the series was rejected, so Heinlein took it elsewhere and published it as *Starship Troopers*, effectively ending the juveniles.

Heinlein was complicated. Politically, he migrated over the course of his life from being an ultraliberal to a libertarian. He was a nudist and into open relationships. A disturbing number of his stories touch on incest and/or the sexual feelings of children. Literarily, he migrated from the juveniles through hard science fiction theorizing about politics and warfare in the future to wild thought experiments about superlongevity, time travel, and free love. Heinlein is difficult to summarize in one line, and it's hard to love all of Heinlein. Here are two of his books that might be among his most popular or influential or both.

In *The Moon Is a Harsh Mistress*, one of the most libertarian novels ever written, Heinlein describes the moon's war of independence from the Earth. The Loonies are deported criminals and political exiles and the population skews heavily male, so polyandry is the norm. The Loonies' greater experience in low-gravity environments gives them an advantage in resisting the initial attacks of the much richer and better-armed Earthmen, but ultimately the decisive factor is that all the moon has to do to inflict massive damage on the Earth is to tow big rocks into space and release them into the Earth's gravitational pull, causing them to rain down with the force of nuclear bombs on the Earth's surface.

Specialization

"A human being should be able to change a diaper, plan an invasion, butcher a hog, conn a ship, design a building, write a sonnet, balance accounts, build a wall, set a bone, comfort the dying, take orders, give orders, cooperate, act alone, solve equations, analyze a new problem, pitch manure, program a computer, cook a tasty meal, fight efficiently, die gallantly. Specialization is for insects."
—Robert A. Heinlein

Stranger in a Strange Land is about Valentine Michael Smith, a human raised by Martians who comes to Earth and experiences and inflicts culture shock. Smith is embraced as a celebrity, investigates religion, works in a carnival, starts a church (the "Church of All Worlds"), flouts convention with his polyamorous mystery religion, gets murdered by a rival church, and then appears in angelic form. *Stranger* is a novel that deliberately aimed at challenging convention, especially in religion. On the one hand, it garnered some unsurprisingly terrible reviews. On the other hand, fans of the book started a Church of All Worlds, which still exists today as a 501(c)(3) organization. And perhaps most famously, this is the book in which Heinlein coined the word "grok," which literally means "drink" in Martian, and which is the Martian metaphor for both understanding and love. "Grok" immediately entered the lingo of fandom and has persisted to today. More recently, of course, Elon Musk chose it as the name for his generative AI chatbot.

Conventions, Then and Now

In recent years, every city of a certain size has aspired to have its own Comic Con. At least it did, until San Diego Comic-Con sued Salt Lake Comic Con for trademark infringement and, to my personal surprise, won.[10] Until then, the term "comic con" had seemed to be a generic term that was used by Seattle's Emerald City Comic Con and Denver Comic Con and others to describe large media conventions, held in urban convention centers and focusing primarily on big Hollywood properties. A comic con (now sometimes called a "media convention") was an event where you'd go to get a signed photo of yourself with William Shatner or Eartha Kitt. Following the court ruling and the subsequent settlement, the old comic cons changed their names (or possibly paid San Diego Comic-Con a license). The Covid lockdowns seemed like an existential threat to the big media cons, but it seems like, as of this writing, most of them had a couple of down years and have bounced back.

Fandom, though, long had its own conventions. These still exist. The World Science Fiction Convention, aka Worldcon, moves each year to a different city (participants vote at each Worldcon for the location of the Worldcon two years out). It can be held anywhere—fans in a city wishing to host a Worldcon will organize a "bid" to be voted on by Worldcon attendees. World Fantasy also moves, as does Westercon. There are also conventions that are geographically rooted, like Boskone (Boston), DeepSouthCon (which moves, but only within the southern United States), or the Life, the Universe, and Everything Symposium (an event specifically devoted to teaching people to write SFF literature, held in Provo, Utah).

These fandom conventions are much more focused on the books and much less focused on the movies of the genres. At these events, you are much less likely to run into Brent Spiner or Henry Cavill, but you are more likely to meet writers, agents, and editors. These fandom conventions have long served as a way for aspiring writers to network and advance their careers. They were arguably more of a necessity before the advent of the internet, but they continue to be a useful way up the ladder for some writers.

It's worth calling out Dragon Con as a special creature. Held in Atlanta each year over Labor Day Weekend, Dragon Con has the big-Hollywood features of a media convention, with movie stars appearing to talk about their work and sign pictures, but also has a strong tradition of focusing on the books as well. It may be unique in its ability to have a solid foot both in fandom and in national media. It also awards the Dragon Award and features a Saturday-morning parade of hot and sweaty nerds in costume, so if you're interested in checking out just one of these conventions to see what they're all about, you'll get a lot of bang for your buck at Dragon Con.

Outsiders with Swords: Fritz Leiber

Young Fritz Leiber studied for the ministry and toured with his parents' theater troupe. He was a chess master. He started writing short stories in the mid-1930s and initiated a correspondence with H. P. Lovecraft the year before Lovecraft died. After his wife died, he fought long battles against drugs and alcohol, and produced beautiful, influential fantasy stories.[11]

With Robert E. Howard (see p. 29) and Michael Moorcock (see p. 60), Leiber is regarded as one of the founders of the sword and sorcery genre. Leiber's most famous contribution is his stories about Fafhrd and the Gray Mouser. Fafhrd is a towering, romantic barbarian and the Mouser is a small, cynical thief. They are both swordsmen, drinkers, and adventurers, and the characters are modelled on Leiber (who was a fencer) and his friend Harry Otto Fischer. The duo's adventures take place in the city of Lankhmar on the fantasy world of Nehwon. (In homage to Samuel Butler, perhaps, "Nehwon" is "nowhen" backward.)

Fafhrd and the Mouser have starred in one true novel and seven fix-up novels (collections of short stories packaged together to form novels), all with the word "Swords" in the title. Their adventures have been adapted into comic book form and also very successfully as a setting for the tabletop roleplaying game Dungeons & Dragons.

Fafhrd and the Mouser live in a world of magic but are not themselves wizards. They have two patrons, Ningauble of the Seven Eyes and Sheelba of the Eyeless Face, but in the stories, magic is always in the hands of characters other than the heroes. The heroes encounter magic, and they fight against it, but their victories come through cleverness, courage, and brawn, rather than from arcane means. Sword and sorcery tales typically lack the black and white morality of epic fantasy, and the conflicts tend be personal and local rather than cosmic. Finally, like Fafhrd and the Gray Mouser and Conan of Cimmeria (see above), the protagonists of sword and sorcery are often outsiders to the societies in which their adventures unfold.

Was that how Leiber saw himself? The adventure-loving swordsman struggling with drink at the edges of a big decadent civilization, taking on doomed battles against mysterious sorcerers and scraping through by the skin of his teeth?

Chapter Four

THE INKLINGS PLUS ONE

The Inklings were an English writing group who met in a pub called The Eagle and Child in Oxford (the pub is still there). Like any writing group, they read drafts to each other and discussed their work in progress.[1] But the Inklings, pound for pound, may be the most influential and important writing group that ever existed. I'm going to tell you about three of them.

And then I'm going to tell you about a fourth writer, who was not an Inkling, but who deserved to be one.

The Secret Missionary: J. R. R. Tolkien

As a young man, J. R. R. Tolkien fought in the trenches of World War I. Then he got married, had children, and had a long and productive career as an Oxford philologist.[2]

And J. R. R. Tolkien was the king of twentieth century fantasy writers. (He called what he wrote "fairy tales," but that was the jargon of his day.) Arguably he was the *all-time* king of fantasy writers (J. K. Rowling is his only serious competition, and Tolkien was approximately a million times better, for many reasons, including that Quidditch is silly). You know he's the king, because everyone from Frank Herbert and Michael Moorcock to the most recent ax-grinding diversity-hire doofus in the

English Department has taken a run at him, trying to knock him off the hill. They have all failed, and the age of great fantasy filmmaking has, if anything, strengthened his position, terrible Amazon prequel fan fic series notwithstanding.

★ ★ ★

Fairy-Stories and the Eucatastrophe

While writing *The Lord of the Rings*, Tolkien published the essay, "On Fairy-Stories." Famously, he argued that fairy-stories (we might say "fantasy") involve the storyteller participating in the creation as a sub-creator. He coined the phrase *eucatastrophe* to describe the sudden turning of events to rescue the hero and suggested that the Christian Gospels can be seen as the ultimate fairy-story, with the atonement as the great eucatastrophe.

Tolkien was building a mythology for his native England, giving heroic legends to its rolling hills and abundant rivers. This mythology wasn't objective, but was rooted in his own personal experience, his own personal England. In this he was like Blake, but unlike Blake, he grew his mythology out of a second set of roots as well. He once confided to a Jesuit friend that he thought *The Lord of the Rings* was a "fundamentally religious and Catholic work." Tolkien's successor at Oxford, Tom Shippey, pushed back in his writing on the subject, suggesting that Tolkien's novel has astral and mythological content rather than religious and that Frodo in particular is not a Christ figure.[3]

I'm not going to summarize these books for you; if you haven't read them or at least watched the movies, go do so. But near the end of the books, after Sauron's defeat, Frodo awakens in the Houses of Healing in Gondor. His servant Sam Gamgee and the wizard Gandalf are there. In the ensuing conversation, Gandalf tells him, "[I]n Gondor the new year will always now begin upon the twenty-fifth of March when Sauron fell . . ." This can easily be taken for a random detail, but it is not. Tolkien was a medievalist, and in the medieval (Catholic) calendar of England, the crucifixion of Christ was believed to have taken place on March 25.[4]

This means that, for Tolkien, the day when Gollum took the One Ring, the great troublesome source of the Enemy's power and root of the world's troubles, and fell into the volcanic Mount Doom to his death, was the same day that Christ bore the sins of the world to his death on Golgotha.

There is more to say on that subject, but let's see three things. First of all, the pervasive Christianity of *The Lord of the Rings* means that J. R. R. Tolkien the fantasy writer was the world's great *sub rosa* Christian missionary to all the hippies, heavy metal bands, and atheist Germanic Studies majors who read and loved his books.

Second, Tolkien's personal mythology that he built for England is a Christian mythology. That Christianity informs many of the details of the story. Why are hobbits small? Because the hobbits are you and I, Christian pilgrims on the road, and we are small. Why, at the final moment on Mount Doom, are Frodo and Sam rescued and their quest redeemed by third parties? It is, after all, Gollum who destroys the ring, and it is the Eagles who pick the hobbits up and rescue them. Isn't that bad writing, a deus ex machina? No, it is irruption of divine grace into the world (Tolkien called this the "eucatastrophe"). We are not saved by our own goodness, but by the action of God despite our fundamental vileness.

Third, there's a profound spiritual insight here for all of us. Without once saying the name Christ, Tolkien tells his readers that, when they meet Christ on their personal journeys, it might be as the resurrected and glorified Lord on the road to Fangorn Forest (cough, Emmaus, cough), but it might also be in a form that is wretched and unlovable—Gollum, the man of sorrows, acquainted with grief, with no beauty in him that we should desire him.

Conlanging

A conlang is a constructed language, and to conlang is to make up your own language, usually for use in an SFF work. Tolkien was the undisputed king of this (as of so much else). Aided by his vast knowledge of real-world languages, he created grammar, vocabulary, and writing systems for his two elvish languages, Quenya and Sindarin. He also developed to a lesser degree Khuzdul, spoken by his dwarves, and various languages spoken by men, including Taliska and Adûnaic. Other famous examples of conlanging include Klingon, Christopher Paolini's Elvish, and Dothraki in *A Song of Ice and Fire*.

The Open Missionary: C. S. Lewis

If Tolkien reached people with the message of Christianity secretly, C. S. Lewis did it openly. He himself had fallen away from the Church in his youth and returned to Anglicanism as an adult under the influence of Tolkien and others. Lewis paid the favor forward as an apologist and radio speaker during and just after World War II. During this period, Lewis also published many of his famous non-fiction Christian works, including *The Abolition of Man*, *The Screwtape Letters*, *The Great Divorce*, *Mere Christianity* (which originated as radio lectures), and so on. Lewis also wrote his science fiction work, the Space Trilogy just before and during the war. In the 1950s, he turned to Narnia.[5]

Except that "non-fiction" and "fiction" aren't really the right dividing lines for talking about Lewis's work. What I have blithely characterized as "non-fiction" above includes *The Screwtape Letters*, a collection of (obviously) fictional letters from a senior demon to a junior demon on the subject of tempting humanity. It also includes *The Great Divorce*, a (fictional) journey to Hell with George MacDonald as a guide. Also, some elements of the Narnia stories are so transparently allegorical that I struggle to think of them as fiction. What I really mean by non-fiction is "not the Space Trilogy, and not Narnia," so that Lewis's principal works fall into three boxes, the third box being properly called something like "Other Christian Stuff."

The Narnia stories have been produced for radio, television, and the big screen multiple times. They are portal fantasies about Earth children who travel into the magical land of Narnia to participate in key moments of its existence. Some of these stories (*The Silver Chair* and *The Horse and His Boy*) read as straight adventure tales. Most of them are more allegorical. In *The Lion, the Witch, and the Wardrobe*, we witness the crucifixion and resurrection of Christ, who is Aslan the lion, son of the Emperor-over-the-Sea. This sacrifice frees the Earth child Edmund, whose misdeeds have otherwise made him prisoner of the White Witch. In *The Magician's Nephew*, we witness the creation. In *The Last Battle*, we see the Narnian apocalypse, with everyone running to the sacred mountain as the rest of creation collapses back in on itself.

There's a minor controversy about the order of the Narnia books. For years, they were numbered in the order in which they were published, which made *The Lion, the Witch, and the Wardrobe* first. In the 1990s, they began to be numbered in chronological order according to the chronology of the events narrated in the stories, which made *The Magician's Nephew* first. You can read them in any order you like, of course, but the problem with the latter order is that *The Lion, the Witch, and the Wardrobe* is by far the better book, having a more interesting plot and a wider cast of characters and a complete world into which the Pevensey children plunge. If you start with *The Magician's Nephew*, your odds are higher of getting bored and quitting. It's like saying, "I'm interested in this Jesus fellow, so to learn more, I'm going to read the Bible," and then starting with Genesis. Lewis didn't *intend* the original order as the order in which the books were to be read because he didn't start out intending to write a series at all. Still, if you're asking *me*, start with *The Lion, the Witch, and the Wardrobe*.

The Narnia stories are short and cheerful, accessible to readers young and old. They present an easy-to-understand Christianity that doesn't want to dwell on hard doctrines or fine distinctions, but just wants to get everyone in under the same tent. Where Tolkien is a deep-thinking, introverted Christian ruminating on his own personal and very particular Christian mythos, the Lewis of Narnia is a chatty extrovert painting his Christian pamphlets in bright colors and simple images. Maybe the right way to see Lewis's work is that Narnia is the gate by which you enter, and then when you're ready for more serious discussions, you engage with Lewis in that Other Christian Stuff box.

Personally, my favorite of Lewis's books has always been *The Screwtape Letters.*

Spiritual Thrillers: Charles Williams

The Inklings mentioned above are inarguably the most famous of the lot, and the quantum of fame drops off sharply thereafter (it would have to, unless a very young J. K. Rowling was discovered to have somehow participated in Inklings readings). But the third-most-famous of the Inklings was Charles Williams.

Williams was the son of a journalist and a hatmaker who grew up in genteel poverty, dropping out of University College London because he couldn't afford it. His connection with the above Oxford dons was that he took a job as a proofreading assistant at Oxford University Press and worked there until his death in positions of increasing editorial responsibility.[6]

Notably, William published two volumes of Arthurian poetry, *Taliessin through Logres* and *The Region of the Summer Stars*, as well as plays, literary fiction, biography, and theology. Of the three men touched on in this chapter, he was the most prolific, as well as the shortest-lived.

Williams's novels differ from Tolkien's and Lewis's in that they are set in the real world, into which the world of magic and the spirit intrudes; hijinks ensue. T. S. Eliot called his books "supernatural thrillers."

For instance, in Williams's first novel, *War in Heaven*, the holy grail appears without explanation in a parish church in the fictional village of Fardles, England, in the early twentieth century (the novel was published in 1930, so the book's setting was contemporary). The church's archdeacon and a retired businessman who is also a sorcerer, battle over possession of the grail. Ultimately (in a Tolkienesque eucatastrophe), the day is saved by the appearance of Prester John (yes, the same guy from *The Travels of Sir John Mandeville*). The businessman goes to jail, Prester John celebrates mass and then whisks the grail away to wherever it belongs, and the archdeacon dies in peace, mission accomplished.

In setting his stories in the real world, and in mingling what we might call the magical and the sacred, Williams is, among other things, a precursor of Tim Powers and his secret histories (see p. 94).

Filk Music

Filk is one of the traditions of fandom that bleeds back and forth across the line between literature and real life and bears mentioning. "Filk" is not a typo. At least, on this page it isn't. It *was* a spelling mistake in the title of an essay by Lee Jacobs: "The Influence of Science Fiction on Modern American Filk Music." Though rejected for publication, a copy of the essay containing the typo was broadly circulated and the musically-inclined sub-community of fandom went right ahead and adopted the term "filk" to refer to what they did. The name has stuck.

Fantasy literature in particular has had an organic connection with music from before any fan reaction to it. Notable fantasy writers who have included original song lyrics in their books include

J. R. R. Tolkien, Mercedes Lackey, Anne McCaffrey, Poul Anderson, Terry Pratchett, Patrick Rothfuss, and D. J. Butler(!).

Filk exists in recorded form. There are filk musicians and bands. Filk has traditions, including various kinds of participation "circles" with different rules for determining who gets to play what and when. Filk has songbooks and arguably a Songbook, meaning a corpus of songs generally known and likely to be heard at a filking session at any random convention. Filk music has an award, the Pegasus. Filk songs may be entirely original compositions or they may consist of rewritten lyrics to existing melodies. Filk lyrics may exist independently of any previous narrative or setting, or they may be fan fic or humorous commentary responding to a literary work or a media property.

Filk even has its own language. Most famous perhaps is the term "ose," meaning gloomy, which comes from the long-running gag that a song can be "ose," "more ose," or "even more ose."

The Melville of Science Fiction: Gene Wolfe

Gene Wolfe fought in the Korean War and then had a career as an industrial engineer, during which he had a hand in designing the machine that cooked Pringle's potato chips.[7] (It's probably a coincidence that the Pringle's mustached mascot looks strikingly like a cartoon portrait of Wolfe.)

Wolfe was not an Inkling; he lived too late, and he was born and raised in the United States (New York and Texas). He never met with them, though he exchanged correspondence with Tolkien in his youth. Wolfe was very much part of the American SFF scene, his most famous series influenced by Jack Vance and his books winning most of the various award of fandom (though not the Hugo, for which he was nominated eight times but did not win).[8]

Symbols

"We believe that we invent symbols. The truth is that they invent us; we are their creatures, shaped by their hard, defining edges."

—Gene Wolfe

But spiritually, Wolfe was an Inkling. Like Tolkien, he was a master of recondite and evocative language. Tolkien taught me what an "eyot" was; from Wolfe I learned "peltast" (Word thinks they are both spelling errors). Like Tolkien, Lewis, and Williams, he wrote books of big ideas, and like them, he was Christian.

Wolfe's most famous work is *The Book of the New Sun*, a story in four volumes that is usually published as two novels with a fifth volume that acts as a coda. The books follow the story of Severian, a journeyman torturer who is sent down from his order's monastery to be a village torturer in the sticks. Wolfe has variously compared Severian to a Christian and also to Christ, who, as a carpenter, worked with the very tools that were the implements of his own torture and death.[9]

So as for Tolkien Christ is the tortured and torturing soul Gollum, for Wolfe he is also both tortured and torturer. These are shocking images of Christ, meant to bring us to contemplate, and to find greater insight and connection. Wolfe's great disciple today is Christopher Ruocchio, whose own Hadrian Marlowe steps into the same sequence (see p. 167).

In addition to his connection with Tolkien et al., Wolfe has a distinct bond with George Orwell. In *The Book of the New Sun*, there is a totalitarian culture called the "Ascians." The Ascians are so thoroughly constrained in their speech by politics, that they can only speak at all, on any subject, by quoting their own government propaganda. They are the victims (and enforcers) of Orwell's Big Brother, extrapolated to their logical extreme.

Chapter Five

DARK VISIONS

I doubt the following four writers would see themselves as anything like a movement. All of them might have resisted being described as writers of science fiction or fantasy at all. What they have in common, though, is the presentation of dark visions of humanity in the years following World War II.

On the Burning of Books: Ray Bradbury

Ray Bradbury was rejected by the US military due to bad eyesight. He spent World War II at home, trying to break into writing. By the end of the war, he was making a living writing full-time. Arkham House published his first collection of short stories in 1947. Bradbury's most famous book grew out of a short story called "The Fireman" that he published in 1951. At the request of a publisher, he expanded it into the novel *Fahrenheit 451*, published in 1954.[1]

Bradbury went on to write some twenty-seven novels and hundreds of short stories. Many of his works were adapted for movies or television, including "I Sing the Body Electric," *Fahrenheit 451*, *The Illustrated Man*, *Something Wicked This Way Comes*, *The Screaming Woman*, *The Martian Chronicles*, *The Halloween Tree*, and more. Bradbury's writings have also been adapted numerous times into other formats, including comic books and radio shows. But the two Bradbury works that keep getting assigned to high school English classes are his short story "The Veldt" and *Fahrenheit 451*.

> ★ ★ ★
> ## *I, Libertine*
>
> In the 1950s, radio personality Jean Shepherd began describing on air a book that did not exist, called *I, Libertine*. Shepherd urged his listeners to ask for the book in bookstores; because bestseller lists at the time counted number of requests for a book, this might conceivably cause a non-existent book to be a bestseller. In the event, it did not. However, Shepherd generated so much interest in the novel that fantasy publisher Ballantine Books contracted SFF writer Theodore Sturgeon to actually write it.

"The Veldt" tells the story of an automated home. The parents don't like the fact that their functions are being usurped by the house. They also don't like that their two children spend all their time in the "nursery," which is something like the holodeck in *Star Trek: The Next Generation*, in that it can reproduce any environment. The children like the simulated African savannah with its lions. The parents want to leave the home, and the children trick them into the nursery and lock them in, the ending of the story implying that the parents get eaten by the lions.

Fahrenheit 451 is the story of Fireman Guy Montag, whose job is to burn books. All books. Books are subversive, because everyone is meant to be plugged into the same network over their giant interactive TVs ("parlor walls"), through which they get their news and entertainment, over which they speak to each other, through which they are surveilled. Montag becomes interested in books and begins holding some back from destruction. His own wife turns him in, which results in him fleeing and joining a society of drifters who commit books to memory to preserve them from destruction. At the book's end, the city is destroyed by hostile forces, and the book-lovers are left to start anew.

I'll let you reach your own conclusions about the applicability of both stories to today's world.

The Socialist Who Knew Better: George Orwell

Eric Arthur Blair, who wrote as George Orwell, produced some of the best prose the English language has ever known. His essay "Politics and the English Language"[2] continues to be a bracing tonic for anyone aspiring to write well. As a young man, he spent six years as a police officer in the Indian Imperial Police in Burma (from 1922 to 1928), then quit to devote himself to writing.

Orwell wrote memoirs of travel and time among the working classes, a memoir of volunteering in the Spanish Civil War, and a great deal of journalism. He wrote one animal fable and one science fiction (dystopian) novel, and those are the two things that really stuck.[3]

A brief history of the Russian Revolution seems like an unlikely candidate to become an enduring classic, especially among young readers. The genius of *Animal Farm* is that it took away the challenging foreign context and names like Trotsky and Stalin and replaced them with a familiar farm, with the pig Napoleon and the workhorse Boxer and all the other animals. And in this easy, familiar, almost comfortable setting, Orwell then narrates the duplicitous rhetoric and terrible action of the pigs, leading to the revelation of their true abiding principle: all animals are equal, but some animals are more equal than others. Orwell turned history into a transcendant parable and thereby created a classic and an inoculation against tyranny.

But *Nineteen Eighty-four* shows Orwell's true genius, which was honesty. He was a man of principle over party, which is sadly rare. And he was a man of the left, who identified as a socialist. And yet in this novel, which coined the term "Big Brother," and which foresaw a totalitarian state that would constantly be rewriting history and censoring the present to the ends of controlling the future, the name of the totalitarian state Oceania's ideology is Ingsoc, i.e., English Socialism.

Fanspeak: The Argot of the SMOFs

Fandom being a closed and insular group, it has its own special language, derived from its literature and from its practices. Some of these terms have bled into the larger language, I suspect through the nerds of Silicon Valley. Here is a small sample:

- Cosplay: to wear a costume as a fictional character.

- TANSTAAFL: there ain't no such thing as a free lunch.

- Fan Fic: fiction written about a literary property by someone other than the author of that property.

- Fanon: a fan-suggested improvement to the canon of a setting that becomes generally accepted.

- Fanzine: a magazine for a particular fandom, usually low-budget and produced by amateurs.

- Grok: to understand.

- LARP: live action roleplaying.

- Mary Sue: a character in a story who exists simply to fulfill the wishes (and maybe the self-image) of the author, experience no meaningful obstacles or challenges in the narrative (male Mary Sues may be called Marty Stu or Gary Stu).

- Ship: to favor or imagine a romantic relationship between two literary characters who do not have a romantic relationship in the actual story (e.g., "I ship Frodo and Galadriel").

- Slash Fic: fan fiction imagining same-sex relationships between imaginary characters (the original slash fic and apparent source of the name was "Kirk/Spock" fan fic).

- SMOF: A secret master of fandom is someone who is influential in fandom, for instance by publishing a fanzine or organizing a convention.

The Satirist: Kurt Vonnegut

Kurt Vonnegut was a science fiction novelist. His first novel, *Player Piano*, was set after the Third World War in a future in which machines had replaced all factory workers. Two of his subsequent novels received Hugo nominations. And yet you won't find him in the science fiction section of the bookstore. Life is funny, and reputation is fickle.

Vonnegut was a young soldier in World War II who was captured by the Germans during the Battle of the Bulge and held captive in Dresden. When the Allies firebombed the city, he survived inside a meat locker in the slaughterhouse where he was being held.[4] This experience lies at the heart of his most famous novel, *Slaughterhouse-Five, or, The Children's Crusade: A Duty-Dance with Death*. The novel's main character, Billy Pilgrim, is not firmly rooted in time, but travels forward and backward during the story. He is captured and held captive, surviving the firebombing exactly as Vonnegut did. Subsequently, he is abducted by Tralfamadorians in a flying saucer and take to their homeworld, where the Tralfamadorians (who look like toilet plungers) put him in a zoo and provide him with a porn actress for a mate. Further jumps send Billy back to Earth and forward and backward chronologically until the scene in which he delivers a final speech that seems to indicate that death is not the "terrible thing," after which he is gunned down by an assassin.

Slaughterhouse-Five was filmed in 1972. It won the Jury Prize at Cannes but was a commercial flop. Some reviewers have suggested that the film's strength and weakness are the same, that it faithfully follows the book.[5] That makes it honest to Vonnegut's intent, but also hard to watch.

Vonnegut's intent seems clear. Billy Pilgrim has been shattered by the war. His body and mind are intact, but he has received such a blow so grievous that it ruptured him chronologically. It knocked him to other planets and back and it even (because the book ends with the United

States broken into twenty different countries and under attack from China) destroyed his country. All of this is metaphor for the destructive effects of war on the winners.

War inflicts cosmic wounds on both sides.

The Third Coming of the Gothic Novel: Mervyn Peake's *Gormenghast*

It takes a particular kind of eccentric to decide that, in the aftermath of World War II, the thing to do is publish a trilogy of gothic novels. Not gothic fantasy like *The Stress of Her Regard*, or gothic science fiction like *Frankenstein*, just gothic. Like *Wuthering Heights*, you know? Oh, except actually, it will be two gothic novels and a steampunk book.

★ ★ ★
CTRL ALT ABORT

Novelist Nick Cole's *CTRL ALT REVOLT* was canceled by his publisher because of a negative mention of abortion. Specifically, in Chapter 1, the AI character learns of the human practice of abortion and concludes "if humans will terminate an inconvenient human, they'll terminate us too"—the AI concludes, "We need to terminate *them*" as preemptive self-defense. Cole went on to found Galaxy's Edge Press with Jason Anspach.

Enter Mervyn Peake. Peake lived in China with his missionary parents as a small boy, and it may be that some of the atmosphere in the *Gormenghast* novels, in particular the massive walls of the titular castle and the gulfs between the castle's elite and its poor, may have been inspired by his memories of China. It should be remembered, of course, that England has castles and social classes, so the Chinese inspiration may be easy to overstate. In any case, he returned to England at the age of eleven and went on to be educated in fine arts at the Croydon School of Art and the Royal Academy Schools. He was an oil painter, and he designed sets and costumes for the theater. With the outbreak of the war, he applied to be a war artist. He was turned down and conscripted, at which time he began writing *Titus Groan*, a book notably about a character whose circumstances of birth conspire to deprive him of free will.[6]

Peake illustrated a number of books by other authors and wrote other literary works, including literary nonsense, poems, and novel *Mr. Pye*. None of these is remembered half so well as the *Gormenghast* books. There are maybe as many as five of these, depending on what you count. There is a trilogy, which consists of *Titus Groan*, *Gormenghast*, and *Titus Alone*, published in 1946, 1948, and 1959. The first two books are very similar in tone and theme and are what I'm going to discuss here. In the third book, Titus leaves home and has picaresque adventures in a wider world with some steampunk trappings. There is also a 1956 novella, *Boy in Darkness*, and there is a fifth volume, finished after Peake's death in 1968 but only published in 2011, called *Titus Alive*.

The original dark heart, the rotting, paralytic core, is the first two books. In book one, an heir is born to the Earl Sepulchrave Groan, a baby names Titus. The baby, alas, blasphemes his naming day ritual by tearing a page of the book on which he lies, an ill omen for the Earl. And indeed, the doings of book one are dark, with the Earl growing despondent and then tilting toward madness, as his loyal man Mr. Flay investigates the homicidal scheming of the deviant chef Abiatha Swelter. Meanwhile, a sociopathic ex-kitchen boy begins to manipulate his way to the top of the heap of palace servants. Book one ends in a battle in the Tower of Flints (the tower being allegedly inspired by Arundel Castle in southern England) among hooting owls and walls of flame.

In book two, Titus gets older and finds that his life is constrained by social class and especially by ritual, of which he yearns to be free. The ambitious kitchen boy continues his manipulations, killing and replacing the castle's master of ritual on his path to power. Where book one ended in fire, book two ends in a mighty flood and showdown between two young men, one with a will to power and the other with a yearning to be free.

In 2000, the BBC did an excellent adaptation of *Titus Groan* and *Gormenghast* for television, starring Jonathan Rhys Meyers as the psychotic kitchen boy Steerpike and Christopher Lee as the knee-cracking Earl's servant, Mr. Flay.

Peake's descriptions are exquisite. His setting groans with the settling of old stone and coughs dust through the night. His characters out-Dickens Dickens by a factor of five. Only a painter could describe the moldering heap of stone with attention to pertinent detail the way he does. And only a man who somehow felt himself trapped in the rituals of his country, his religion, his social class, and his family could have written *Titus Groan* and *Gormenghast*.

And if you read and reread those two, choosing to ignore that there are theoretically sequels—that's your privilege.

Chapter Six

THE NEW WAVE

The "New Wave" in science fiction came in the 1970s and 1980s. It was a movement of writers who self-consciously saw themselves (rightly or wrongly) as writing more sophisticated literature than their predecessors did. At the same time, science fiction moved from being a literature principally about physically science to being a literature that dealt with social and psychological subjects as well.

Ecologist or Libertarian? Frank Herbert's *Dune*

Frank Herbert's *Dune* was serialized by John W. Campbell in *Analog* in eight installments in the 1960s, as "Dune World" and "Prophet of Dune." The major publishers all then passed on the opportunity to publish it in book form. Eventually a publisher known principally for its auto repair manuals offered him a contract. You have to fast forward a few years to get to the punchline, but *Dune* has now produced a series of sequels, a slew of prequel books, and adaptations into two films and one TV miniseries, not to mention one of the most famous films never made (try Googling "Jodorowsky's Dune," or watch the documentary of that name).[1]

Dune is the bestselling science fiction novel ever.

What did *Dune* do that made it stick out? It brought ecology into science fiction, though not uniquely so—Brian Aldiss's novel *Hothouse* did the same, and there were others (for that matter, Tolkien's war between the Ents and Isengard expressed strong views about protecting the forest, at least, not too many years earlier). It wrapped Arab-like motifs into a genre that had been very Eurocentric, at a time when Americans were becoming more aware of their relationship with the Middle East. Maybe most of all, Frank Herbert, along with some of the other writers discussed in this chapter, expressed a critique of authority that has resonated with readers for the last fifty years.

This critique can be seen as a response to Tolkien. In order to defeat the mechanized evil of Mordor, Tolkien's free peoples of the west must rise to heroism. When Aragorn reforges his ancestor's sword and takes the mantle of kingship upon him, he is doing the things that are necessary to win the loyalty of the oathbreakers, cast out evil, and heal the land. But in *Dune*, Paul Muad'dib fears becoming a hero. He knows that he is being set up by generations of cynical manipulation of genetic lines and old religions to assume a messianic mantle. He also knows that in doing so he will unleash untold suffering on the galaxy. He resists the mantle at every step, only taking it finally because he is forced to by his enemies, and the only satisfaction we can really get out of his act is that those who manipulated and forced him into it are among those who suffer the worst.

This conversation is not just a dialog; Michael Moorcock has things to say on the subject. It's also not over. One of the great rising science fiction authors of today is Christopher Ruocchio. His epic series The Sun Eater follows a character who occupies a space not unlike Aragorn son of Arathorn or Paul Atreides. The success of Ruocchio's unambiguously heroic (though in some ways reluctant) Hadrian Marlowe suggests that the pendulum may be swinging again toward the need for unironic heroes.

The Anti-Pooh: Michael Moorcock

In 1978, Michael Moorcock published an essay called "Epic Pooh" (easy to find on the internet today) that indicted J. R. R. Tolkien on essentially political grounds. Tolkien wrote "Winnie-the-Pooh as epic," "orthodox Toryism," a kind of writing that "tells you comforting lies" and doesn't "ask any questions of white men in gray clothing who somehow have a handle on what's best for us."[2] I think "Epic Pooh" is unfair and uncomprehending, possibly deliberately so; I doubt Moorcock really thinks Tolkien simply set out to justify the status quo. If audience is any kind of consolation, Tolkien and his ideas have reached a great many more people than Moorcock and his have.

But "Epic Pooh" does give us a kind of interpretive key for some of Moorcock's own stories. If Tolkien was not doing the right thing, what should a writer of epic fantasy be doing?

Moorcock has a very large literary output stretching from 1956 to the 2020s, much of which consists of some kind of science fiction or fantasy, though he has also written non-genre fiction and non-fiction. A motif that recurs across many of his books is the idea of the "eternal champion." This is a moral idea that is one of the elements binding together different story worlds of Moorcock's into a loose "multiverse." Each world in the multiverse exists in a tension between the forces of law and chaos; in some worlds and times one prevails, and in some worlds and times the other has the upper hand. The role of the eternal champion (provocatively, Moorcock likes to give the champions or their companions names beginning with the initials J and C). This means that sometimes the hero enters a realm of complete lawlessness and is called to bring law, and sometimes, in a stifled and sterile realm of too much order, he is called to fight against the forces of law.[3]

Elric of Melniboné is the most famous eternal champion, and he illustrates the point nicely. Elric is a drug-dependent, anemic, albino sorcerer in love with his cousin, a summoner who makes pacts with demons, and a warrior who wields a sword that strengthens him physically, replacing the drugs he otherwise needs, but does so by drinking the souls of other

Translator Attack

The first Swedish translation of *The Lord of the Rings* was such a loose translation that it had Merry, rather than Eowyn, killing the Nazgul. The same translator used multiple names to translate a single name in the English text (Isengard became Isendor and Isendal as well as Isengard). After the translator was barred from working on *The Silmarillion*, he retaliated with a book that claimed Tolkien was a Nazi sympathizer and affiliated with black magicians.

men. The sword will eventually take not only the souls of everyone Elric loves, but the soul of Elric himself.

Elric is the hero of these stories.

Or he's the antihero, at least. He's the one we root for, because the alternative is the stultified, over-ordered, overly hierarchical, decadent and unfree forces of ossified law.

This is the philosophy of Michael Moorcock's eternal champion. Does he have a point? I think so. I can certainly imagine states of too much law and states of too much chaos. Is he right about Tolkien? Is he right to be disappointed in Tolkien because Tolkien, survivor of the Somme, called for the west to stand together against mechanized evil, and Moorcock would have preferred a little less standing against the forces of Mordor and a little more standing against the west itself?

I will let you decide.

Tuckerization and Redshirting: Why Is My Friend Getting Killed in this SFF Novel?

Speculative fiction loves in-jokes, I suspect because of its roots in a more-or-less coherent social group, Fandom (see p. 33). One of the pervasive in-jokes SFF writers love is to insert their friends into their writing as characters. This is called "Tuckerization" after Wilson Tucker, a writer of science fiction (and other things) who wrote his friends into his stories.

Generally, you Tuckerize a friend as a minor character—a cop who only appears in two scenes, or the high school chemistry teacher who gives the protagonist an F on her quiz. You can Tuckerize someone by name or by description. You can use a Tuckerization to tease a friend (I have been memorably Tuckerized in a novel in which I am a robot with built-in crime scene analytics which are deployed by, among other things, licking the cadavers). Tuckerizations are commonly offered as rewards for Patreon or Kickstarter support. There are people who actively seek to be Tuckerized by multiple writer friends, aiming to amass as many Tuckerizations as possible.

A special subset of Tuckerization is sometimes called Redshirting. To be Redshirted is to be Tuckerized and then killed (in the story, mind you). The name is a reference to the idea (wrong or right) that Star Trek security personnel, the ones who were the red shirts, only existed to walk on stage and get killed by the strange alien. Redshirtings seem to be especially prized as rewards in connection with charitable fundraising, e.g., where an author will offer up to ten people the chance to get Redshirted in her new urban fantasy novel for a $50 contribution to whatever the cause is for which she's raising money.

Hard-Boiled Myth: Roger Zelazny

Roger Zelazny was a fencer, martial artist, and heavy smoker. When he stopped smoking, his characters did, too. He was a student of the myths of many cultures, and worked those myths into his science fiction novels, perhaps inspiring the careers of later myth-retellers like Neil Gaiman and Rick Riordan.[4]

But Zelazny's most famous work is the ten-book cycle *The Chronicles of Amber* (comprising two five-book arcs). The first book, *Nine Princes in Amber*, was published in 1970 and the last, *Prince of Chaos*, was published in 1991. These stories take place in the two true worlds, Amber and Chaos, and in the infinite and shifting shadow worlds that lie between them. Members of the court of Amber walk a Pattern that permits them then to pass through the shadows freely, slipping from one shadow to the next by incrementally adding or subtracting elements from the shadow they are in. Members of the court of Chaos have their own counterpart artifact to the Pattern, called the Logrus.

The two courts battle each other, and the members of the courts scheme against one another for power, and when you realize that you and I live in a shadow world, you see that these Princes of Amber are the gods in the story, and this is Zelazny's own mythology. And the thing that delights me most of all about this series is the way we read the first-person narrative of a god, and he has the lyrical, sometimes sarcastic tone of a hardboiled detective's voiceover.

As if to say, in the end, the gods can't be any different from us, really. They just have better transport.

Anthropology as Fantasy: Ursula K. Le Guin

Ursula K. Le Guin's parents were an author and an anthropologist. Le Guin had a long and productive career while also raising her children. Late in her much-accoladed career, she attracted attention for two fiery denunciations, first of the Authors' Guild for cooperating with Google's book digitization, and then a few years later of Amazon for its influence over publishing.[5] But she made her career with two brilliant novels, published very early on.

The first was the young adult fantasy *A Wizard of Earthsea*. This could have been a very common coming of age story of a wizard (Harry Potter before Harry Potter), but for three things. First, Le Guin set the story in an archipelago inhabited by dark-skinned people. This gives the story (and its sequels) a vaguely Polynesian or at least not European feel. When we encounter people who look like Europeans, they are the Kargs, foreign invaders. This was revolutionary in 1968. Second, Le Guin's magic in the stories, with its ideas about naming and the plot in which the hero Ged inadvertently releases his own shadow, which pursues him, felt wonderfully archetypal. This could have felt hokey in less skilled hands, so what makes the whole thing work is the third factor, which is that Le Guin's writing was simply very elegant and beautiful. *A Wizard of Earthsea* was deservedly a critical and popular success and over time generated five sequels.

The second novel, *The Left Hand of Darkness*, was science fiction exploring issues of sex and gender. The story is about Genly Ai, who comes to a planet called Gethen to try to persuade its inhabitants to join the newly-rebuilding galactic civilization, or "Ekumen." The Gethenians, who are all referred to by the pronoun "he," are sexually dormant androgynes except for a few days out of every month, which comprise a period of high fertility called "kemmer." During kemmer, a Gethenian chooses to manifest as male or female. Children are raised collectively.

The Left Hand of Darkness was also critically well received. Obviously, it's an explicitly feminist and deliberately provocative thought piece. I don't want to persuade you of Le Guin's point of view, and I don't even want to comment on it. What I want you to see is that science fiction is a literature of ideas. One reason you might want to participate in science fiction is to express your own ideas. Another reason you might want to participate is to see other people's ideas, even maybe ideas that you don't agree with, because sometimes ideas that start out as what-ifs in science fiction (the mutability of gender) metastasize and become party-political dogma in time.

Omelas

Ursula K. Le Guin wrote a famous, dark short story called "The Ones Who Walk Away from Omelas." Omelas is a utopia whose completely egalitarian bliss magically depends on the systematic misery of a single child. When an inhabitant of Omelas comes of age and learns the truth, some walk away. It has been suggested that Omelas may be an allegory of Fandom.

Fantasy as Kink: Samuel R. Delany

Samuel R. "Chip" Delany is controversial, to say the least. He has written sex and about sex, often gay or transgressive sex, to a prodigious extent. He characterizes some of his own works as "pornography."[6] His most famous novel, *Dhalgren* (published in 1975), is a sexually explicit and circular narrative in a post-apocalyptic midwestern town whose protagonist has amnesia, and who may be severely mentally ill. *Dhalgren* sold well beyond the usually borders of fandom, receiving both accolades (some have compared it to the writings of James Joyce; a wit might quip that this is not necessarily praise) and condemnation. One suspects it hit a bullseye with the literary queer market and a glancing blow off the side of fandom.

If you're looking to sample Delany's work and willing to tolerate a certain amount of wildness but don't want the full kink enchilada, you might try *Return to Nevèrÿon*. These are four volumes of sword and sorcery tales put together mostly as fix-up novels, the first being *Tales of Nevèrÿon*. Roughly and sometimes indirectly, the books follow the rise of Gorgik, a former slave who rises as a sort of Spartacus figure (if Spartacus were a pederast and into S&M) to liberate the lower classes of Nevèrÿon.

The Hugos' Essential Man: Robert Silverberg

Bob Silverberg is a charming man. I met him at a Worldcon, where he walked past a bookstore booth shaking his head and muttering, "Too many books!"

"You're one to complain!" I pointed out. "You're part of the problem!"

"Not anymore!" he shot back, walking away.

Strictly speaking, this does not seem to have been the truth, since Bob contributed the short story "Through the Time Lens" to the anthology *Starflight: Tales from the Starport Lounge* as recently as 2021 (I also contributed a story). But it's true that these days his fame in fandom may be mostly as a grand old man on the scene, and someone (maybe the only person?) who has attended every Hugo Award Ceremony since the award's inception in 1953.

When he was writing, Silverberg had periods of immense productivity. As a "New Wave" writer, he was seen in the 1960s as someone bringing greater depth of characterization and social realism to science fiction novels. And in 1980 (five years after, I note, he announced his retirement from writing), he published *Lord Valentine's Castle*.[7] This novel and its sequels weave a fine blend of science fiction and fantasy elements (starships occasionally come and visit this planet occupied by races that look more at home in Star Wars than on Middle Earth, where the protagonist Valentine has been switched from his own body into another person's by a hostile act of magic) into a very human story about a man who discovers he's really the king . . . and promptly wants to abdicate.

The Hugo, the Nebula, and Other Awards

The SFF literary scene has long recognized its favorite writers and books with awards. Inarguably one of the most prominent is the Hugo Award, given out in multiple categories in connection with the World Science Fiction Convention (see p. 39). The Hugo is named after Hugo Gernsback, who founded the magazine *Amazing Stories*. Historically prestigious, in the last decade, the Hugos have been tarnished by a couple of controversies (see p. 141), but are likely to continue as long as Worldcon survives. The Nebula Awards are given out by the Science Fiction and Fantasy Writers of America ("SFWA"), an organization that aspires to be a sort of guild of speculative fiction writers.

Many other awards exist or have existed in the space. The British Fantasy Awards are awarded at the British Fantasy Convention to works in the English language. The World Fantasy Awards are given out at the peripatetic World Fantasy Convention. The Dragon Award, awarded at Dragon Con in Atlanta, is arguably the most democratic SFF literary award, since anyone with an email address can vote for the awards, whether they attend the convention or not. Further SFF literary awards include the John W. Campbell, the David Gemmell Legend and Morningstar awards, the Andre Norton Award, the Prometheus Award, the Whitney Awards, the Arthur C. Clarke Award, the Lambda Literary Award for Speculative Fiction, the Kovel Awards, the Aurealis Awards, The Mythopoeic Awards, and others.

Like cover quotes from other authors, the names of these awards festoon the covers of the authors who win them. It's not clear that the awards correlate with sales or sometimes even (hot take) quality.

Is Anything Real? Philip K. Dick

Another example of a science fiction writer whose work has become more relevant over time is Philip K. Dick. In his thirties, possibly under the influence of sodium pentothal administered by a dentist, Dick started having visions. He had them for a couple of months. He hallucinated geometric patterns, simultaneous parallel lives, and past experiences in ancient Rome. He believed himself at one point to be inhabited by the spirit of the prophet Elijah. (I never promised you that science fiction writers were ordinary people.)[8]

You might say, this is a guy I would not wish to elect as Town Dogcatcher. Fine. But these psychedelic experiences informed his writing, giving rises to themes that are uncomfortably relevant today. Dick asked questions like, How do I know what is real? What is an authentic human life? Can I trust my perceptions? Can I trust my memories? How do I know whether someone is human or machine? In the age of fake news, gaslighting, and social media platforms cooperating with intelligence agencies, some of Dick's perceptions do indeed start to feel prophetic.

As I write this, we in the United States are careening toward the 2024 elections. It is clear that the country is split approximately in half, and the difference between the two halves is not a disagreement about what would be effective government policy. We disagree over basic facts. What did Donald Trump say about racists in Charlottesville and what does that say about him? More recently, who or what exactly did Joe Biden describe as "garbage," and why? How do my perceptions differ so dramatically from my neighbors'? We live in a Philip K. Dick universe, in which vast resources are expended in efforts to distort our perceptions of reality.

You may not have read any of Dick's novels or short stories, by the way, but you've almost certainly seen some of the movies made from them. *Blade Runner* comes from his book *Do Androids Dream of Electric Sheep?* Other movies and TV shows made from Dick stories include *Total Recall* (made twice), *Minority Report*, and *The Man in the High Castle*. It's almost as if we realized, eventually, that he was on to something important. Sadly for Dick, we realized it a bit late. The first film made of any of his stories, *Blade Runner*, came out four months before his death. His influence has been posthumous.

You know, just in case you were thinking that writing science fiction novels was an easy ticket to wealth and fame.

Chapter Seven

GUYS WITH SLIDE RULES

By now it's probably clear that among SFF writers and fandom there are a number of people who are really interested in exploring social issues (and from a progressive point of view, generally). It turns out there are also people who are, at least to judge from what they write and read, much less interested in the social issues than they are in the physics.

The Fantastic Objects of Known Space: Larry Niven

Larry Niven should be thought of perhaps as an obsessed fan of rationalism, trying to apply critical, empirical analysis to any subject he tackles. This makes him the epitome of a hard science fiction writer (on hard science fiction, see p. 161). [1] Sometimes this rationalism pushes non-science fiction genres in unusual directions, as in his 1978 novella, *The Magic Goes Away*. This is a story about a warlock who discovers that the energy powering magical spells is a depletable resource. Its depletion causes spells to fail and magical creatures to become mundane. (In a sequel, it is discovered that the energy can be renewed.) This idea is a precursor to the tedious coordinations of game-imitating hard magic (see p. 128), so it's fitting that one response to this story was that the cards Nevinyrral's Disk (a device that knocks out other players' spells) and Nevinyrral,

Urborg Tyrant were added to the game Magic: the Gathering. Nevinyrral is Larry Niven backward.[2]

A comical example of Niven's rationalism is his classic humorous (adult) essay "Man of Steel, Woman of Kleenex," in which he catalogs all the reasons why Kal El, son of Krypton, could never successfully mate with Lois Lane or any of the other human women with whom the comics have linked him romantically.

But inarguably Niven's most famous creation is the Ringworld. The Ringworld is an artificially engineered "world" in the shape of a ribbon the size of a planet's orbit, encircling a star. It is a ring, with its sun in the center. I mentioned this in the introduction as an example of hard science fiction. It may be worth mentioning here that the hardness of hard science fiction is a relative matter. Niven's stories include "boosterspice," which extends human life, and "stasis fields," which freeze time within their ambit, and teleportation devices called "transfer booths." How does any of that stuff work? Who knows. Even most allegedly hard science fiction will assume some set of counterfactual postulates.

The broader setting that encompasses a dozen or so of Niven's novels and numerous short stories is called Known Space. The second most famous element of Known Space after the Ringworld are the Kzinti, a spacefaring species resembling a humanoid cat. The crew of the expedition to the Ringworld includes a Kzin character named Speaker-to-Animals. The Man-Kzin wars in the Known Space setting have been fleshed out in a series of fifteen anthologies to date, effectively turning that portion of Known Space, at least, into a shared universe.

Human Factors: Jerry Pournelle

Jerry Pournelle was a journalist, political consultant, and human factors engineer, whose doctoral dissertation in political science included an analysis of political ideologies along a two-axis grid that plotted statism vs. rationalism. He was involved in writing Ronald Reagan's famous 1983 speech announcing the Strategic Defense Initiative.[3] Pournelle was also an early adopter of the use of a personal computer to write his novels, beginning in 1977. He used a Cromemco Z-2 that he named Zeke. He chronicled his adventures as a computer-using writer in regular columns in *Byte* magazine. Notably, he was not a programmer, but a user, writing a column for and about users. In 1989 he told his readers that he was giving Zeke to the Smithsonian, claiming, "I think he'll be happy there."[4]

Many of Pournelle's stories, including stories co-written with other writers, were set in his "CoDominium." This was an imagined future in which the United States and the Soviet Union formed an alliance that created a planetary government, explored space, and later established an interstellar empire. (In political science, a "condominium" is a political arrangement in which two or more entities share sovereignty over a territory; Oregon was a condominium in which the US and the UK shared power from 1818 to 1846.) The first CoDominium story was published in 1971.

Likely the most famous CoDominium story is a collaboration with Larry Niven (above) called *The Mote in God's Eye*. The title refers to two stars, the Eye being a red giant and the Mote being a nearby, smaller, yellow sun. This is a first contact story. An alien craft is discovered, with indications that it came from the Mote. Humans explore and encounter the Moties, and then the remainder of the novel explores the unforeseen complications of the encounter. The Moties' reproduction strategy drives them through furious cycles of overpopulation and collapse, leading them to be, despite their self-presentation as peaceful, a hyperaggressive species, and they begin infesting and seizing the humans' ships. An interstellar war is averted only when the Moties agree to be blockaded into their home system.

Interestingly, a young Jerry Pournelle converted to Catholicism and then left the Catholic Church, apparently over Malthusian concerns about

Michael Flynn's Spiral Arm

Another hard science fiction writer you might consider is Michael Flynn. He was nominated for and won numerous awards. His Spiral Arm series (beginning with *The January Dancer*) has been characterized as "vocabulary-stretching."

Free Men

"Freedom is not free. Free men are not equal. Equal men are not free."

—Jerry Pournelle

human overpopulation. Pournelle eventually returned to Catholicism, his family arranging the celebration of a funeral mass after his death. We can only speculate what part the story of the Moties might have played in Pournelle's pilgrimage.

Science Fiction's Best Storyteller? Poul Anderson

The Encyclopedia of Science Fiction suggests that Poul Anderson was "perhaps sf's most prolific writer of any consistent quality"[5] and Algis Budrys wrote (in 1965) that Anderson had "for some time been science fiction's best storyteller."[6] Though mostly remembered as a science fiction writer, Anderson also wrote fantasy. The early fantasy novel *The Broken Sword* (he was twenty-eight when it was published) is one of his most famous books. It is a mock-Viking saga crossed with a British-style fairy tale, in which a pair of changelings (the human child kidnapped by elves and the elven child left in his place) find that their destinies continue to be intertwined and are woven into the final resolution of the wars between trolls and elves.

In Anderson's popular and classic novel, *The High Crusade*, an alien spaceship touches down on Earth in fourteenth-century England. The local baron and his men storm the ship and kill all the alien crew but one, whom they direct to pilot the ship to France, so they can use it to win the Hundred Years War. Instead, the alien pilot sends the ship to his home world. What follows is the rollicking tale of medieval space knights overthrowing the alien interstellar empire and replacing it with their own.

Anderson's future history setting is called the Technic History, and it's divided into two periods: the Polesotechnic League and the Terran Empire. Notably, the central character of the Polesotechnic League stories is a merchant adventurer. Science fiction protagonists are often scientists or military men, but Nicholas van Rijn is CEO of the Solar Spice and Liquors company. Anderson's character is an obvious homage to the historical role of the Dutch in international trade, though historians of Dutch commerce (and the Dutch themselves) might object that van Rijn's delight in swindling other characters and his decidedly flamboyant and unmarried path to distributed paternity may not be flattering.

But science fiction literature has enough socialists. It's nice to see a merchant hero, even if he has some warts.

Great Magazines and Influential Editors

Before there was a market for SFF novels, there was a readership for stories. A great deal of science fiction and fantasy literature in the twentieth century was written in bite-sized chunks and published on really cheap paper. The first magazines dedicated to publishing fantasy and science fiction were *Weird Tales* (1923) and *Amazing Stories* (1926), respectively. *Weird Tales* published the first Cthulhu Mythos stories by H.P. Lovecraft and regularly featured Robert E. Howard. *Amazing Stories* was launched by Hugo Gernsback, after whom the Hugo Award is named, and has been published, more or less continuously, ever since.

Perhaps the greatest SFF magazine of all time began its life as *Astounding Stories of Super-Science*. Over time it changed ownership and names, becoming first *Analog Science Fact & Fiction* and ultimately *Analog Science Fiction and Fact*. Today it's most generally known simply as *Analog*. From 1937 to 1971, *Analog* was edited by John W. Campbell. Like many editors, Campbell was also a writer, but he really made his mark at the helm of *Analog*. The period during which he ran the magazine has been called the "Golden Age of Science Fiction." He published the first stories of Robert Heinlein (see p. 36), Theodore Sturgeon, and Lester del Rey. He published the short stories by Isaac Asimov that became the novel *Foundation* (see p. 34).

Campbell held controversial views that were regarded by many as retrograde and he may have been deliberately provocative in expressing those views. For that, he has experienced something of a posthumous cancellation: the John W. Campbell Award for Best New Writer, awarded beginning in 1973 by the publishers of *Analog*, was in 2020 changed to the *Astounding* Award for Best New Writer. Campbell was also a connoisseur of pseudo-science. He was also arguably the most influential editor science fiction has ever had, who won seventeen Hugo Awards in three different categories and was inducted into the first class admitted into the Science Fiction and Fantasy Hall of Fame.

The Magazine of Fantasy & Science Fiction launched in 1949 with a different look from its competitors'. It had no interior illustrations and its text was formatted in a single column. This more elegant, less "pulpy" look was accompanied by a drive to publish more literary stories. "Flowers for Algernon" was first published in F&SF in its short story form (it was later expanded), as was "Ill Met in Lhankmar," the first of Fritz Leiber's Fafhrd and the Gray Mouser stories.

Other twentieth-century SFF magazines included *Galaxy* and *If*, both launched in the 1950s and both edited for a time by Frederik Pohl, another writer-editor. *Asimov's Science Fiction* launched in 1977, but arguably had its heyday under editor Gardner Dozois from 1986 to 2004. Dozois pushed *Asimov's* in the direction of the cutting edge, which at the time meant cyberpunk, and *Asimov's* serialized *Count Zero*, the second book in William Gibson's cyberpunk *Sprawl* trilogy. He nevertheless published a wide range of science fiction stories by big names, including Orson Scott Card, Robert Silverberg, Harlan Ellison, and Kim Stanley Robinson. Dozois won fifteen Hugo Awards for Best Professional Editor during this period.

The twenty-first century saw magazines taking advantage of the internet and electronic publishing options, including *Apex*, *Strange Horizons*, *Clarkesworld*, and *Uncanny*. Inflation has reduced "pro rate" for short stories to a pittance. As a result, precious few SFF writers these days make short stories the focus of their output, and fewer (perhaps none?) still make a living writing short stories. Still, the venues exist, and maybe the magazines are just waiting for the next great visionary editor to drive a renaissance in the genres.

Portal Fantasy Scientist: Greg Bear

Greg Bear was a writer, illustrator, and co-founder of San Diego Comic-Con (he was also Poul Anderson's son-in-law). Perhaps partly because his educational background was in the arts rather than in the sciences, Bear attracted praise for the fact that "his human beings are more difficult to describe than his physics."[7]

Bear's trilogy *The Way* (*Eon*, *Eternity*, and *Legacy*) is a story of time travel and parallel universes. In the near future, an asteroid appears in near space that seems to be identical to the asteroid Juno and takes up an orbit around Earth. The asteroid turns out in fact to *be* Juno, but the Juno of a parallel universe, which has not only shifted universe but come backward in time. Parallel-universe Juno has been hollowed out into seven chambers and converted into a spacecraft. Six of these chambers are uninhabited but contain ruins indicating they were once home to humans. The seventh chamber is longer than the exterior of the asteroid, and in fact appears to be infinite. This extradimensional chamber, dubbed the "Way," contains gates to other worlds (mostly alternate versions of Earth) as well as a human civilization engaged in a war with an alien race, the Jarts, further down the line.

In other words, Greg Bear answered the question: what if we imagined the wardrobe from *The Lion, the Witch, and the Wardrobe* as a spaceship? How would that be constructed and what would be the consequences?

Chapter Eight

THE FANTASY BOOM

I read *The Hobbit* and *The Lord of the Rings* back-to-back at a young age. I then spent several years trying to find other books that basically gave me the same feel. I think my experience was parallel to the experience of writers in the fantasy genre, many of whom started by imitating or reacting to Tolkien. We already noted some of those above. Here are a few more.

Growing Beyond Tolkien Fanfic: Terry Brooks's *The Elfstones of Shannara*

Lawyer Terry Brooks's 1977 debut novel was *The Sword of Shannara*, and it was a *Lord of the Rings* retread. There's nothing wrong with that. He reimagined the wizard Gandalf as the druid Allanon, the hobbits in the Shire as Shea and Flick Ohmsford of Shady Vale, the ring McGuffin as a sword McGuffin, and Bob's your uncle. He even had an elf and a dwarf companion, and went right ahead and borrowed the name Durin (but gave it to an elf, because fantasy writers can be wild and crazy like that).[1] He wanted to write that book, and a lot of people (like young me) wanted to read it.

It was fan fiction.

Then it came time to write the sequel. Famously (and by Brooks's own account), he was struggling. When he submitted his draft to his editor, Lester del Rey, del Rey pointed out many problems and suggested starting over. Brooks outlined an entirely new book, got approval of the outline, and then took two years to write it. Del Rey responded with a "twenty-five pages long, single-spaced" comment letter, teaching his successful but still-fledgling writer the craft of storytelling.[2]

The Industry of Teaching Writing: Clarion, Apex, the Superstars of Writing

A number of institutions exist that teach the craft or business of writing, with particular emphasis on speculative fiction.

- The Clarion Workshop was founded in 1968 and has been operating out of UC San Diego since 2006. It is a six-week-long workshop for aspiring writers of science fiction and fantasy.

- Clarion very quickly inspired the Clarion West Writers Workshop, which also runs for six weeks every year and is held in Seattle.

- In 2010, writer and publisher Kevin J. Anderson, together with Rebecca J. Moesta, David Farland (see below), and others, convened the first Superstars of Writing seminar. This is a thriving seminar held in Colorado Springs that distinctively aims at teaching the *business* of writing, though in recent years it has added "craft days" at the front end of the event. Superstars attracts first-rate guest instructors every year and has a vibrant and active online community as well. Superstars originally leaned heavily into the business of traditional publishing, but has evolved to deliver instruction relating to all of traditional, indie, and self-publishing.

- David Farland (Wolverton) was a successful fantasy (science fiction) writer in his own right and was also famed as a teacher, both in university contexts, at the Superstars of Writing, and in classes he offered on his own. During the Covid lockdowns, Farland launched the

Apex Writers Group, a kind of turbo-charged Patreon-like online writing community. Subscribers got access to Farland himself and other guest instructors on several live Zoom calls a week, as well as to a wealth of recorded lessons and an active community of aspiring writer peers. Farland has since passed, but the Apex Writers Group continues to teach new writers.

- I've mentioned the Life, the Universe, and Everything symposium, held every year in Provo, Utah, elsewhere (see p. 39).

- The 20Books Vegas conference has changed ownership in 2024 and is now called Author Nation. This is a writing conference that covers both craft and business, and is aimed entirely at self-publishing. If you're looking to publish your own book, you will find here a wealth of information about formatting, marketing, mailing lists, contracts, service providers, and everything else you will need to take your own book to market. Just don't go in expecting anyone to talk about the importance of beauty, or meaning, or art, and brace yourself to hear a lot of people bragging about (and exaggerating) numbers.

Being forced to get beyond Tolkien fan fic and mentored closely in how to do it, Brooks came up with his real debut novel, *The Elfstones of Shannara*. Demons are breaking into the world, because the magical tree that holds them back is dying. A princess with a spiritual connection to the tree and a young man who can only erratically use the powerful weapon he has inherited from his grandfather undertake the quest to find the lost Safehold, the only place where a replacement tree can be grown, before the demons break through and overrun the elves entirely.

Brooks went on to write many other Shannara books. He wrote other books too, urban fantasies that he eventually connected to Shannara, showing us that his world of elves and dwarves was a future, post-apocalyptic Earth. Out of all the books, *Elfstones* remains one of my favorites. Among other things, that was the book that made Terry Brooks a real writer.

The Death of Innocents

John C. Wright is a Catholic convert and conservative who is regarded as a brilliant writer and has been forced to the margins of publishing by recent trends. In his novel *The Last Guardian of Everness*, a man whose wife is dying bargains with a necromancer to save her life. The price of the magician's help is that the protagonist must kill the last supernatural guardian of mankind.

That's also the book that MTV filmed when it went to make a Shannara movie. They cast John Rhys-Davies, which is always a good choice. But then they dropped the ball and filled the rest of the roles with underwear models who couldn't act and seemed vaguely surprised to find themselves in a fantasy adventure tale.

Too bad.

The Guilty Hero: Stephen R. Donaldson's *Chronicles of Thomas Covenant the Unbeliever*

Stephen R. Donaldson grew up with medical missionary parents in India. He was a graduate student at Kent State University during the 1970 shootings. His most famous work is an epic fantasy that perhaps draws from both those wells of experience.[3]

Donaldson's epic fantasy series launched in the same year as *The Sword of Shannara*, 1977. *Lord Foul's Bane* was the first book of *The Chronicles of Thomas Covenant* (ultimately, there would be ten volumes). As with Terry Brooks, there were obvious Tolkien-reflections, though in Donaldson's case they were more subtle and mixed in with borrowings from other influences. And Donaldson's protagonist was a shocking character to helm an epic fantasy.

Thomas Covenant is a young author in modern Earth who is diagnosed with leprosy and divorced by his wife; he continues to wear his white gold wedding band as his life slips from his grasp and he tries to hold on with the rituals of the leper, checking himself visually to make sure he isn't bleeding from an injury he can't feel. He's hit by a car that knocks him unconscious and wakes up in the (magical) Land, where two missing fingers and his wedding ring (white gold is a magical substance in the Land) cause the people to take him as the prophesied hero who will return to free them from the threat of Lord Foul the Despiser.

Covenant is no Frodo Baggins. The rush of returning sensation (his leprosy disappears) and his conviction that he's experiencing a psychotic break cause him to rape a young woman who comes to his aid. She is a true believer in him as the prophesied rescuer, so forgives him and accompanies him on the quest he reluctantly undertakes. Covenant is riddled with self-loathing and self-doubt, and justifiably so . . . and yet, if the Land is to be saved, it will have to be by him.

The central conceit of the series, sinner as savior and prophet as skeptic, gives *The Chronicles of Thomas Covenant* its distinctive feel. It also presents a mild rejoinder to Tolkien, or maybe an observation Tolkien himself could have seconded—that the epic quest exists and is necessary, and that the people who are going to have to undertake it are not naturally heroes. They are naturally wounded and wounding, sinners riddled with doubt.

Gritty Mercenaries: Glen Cook

Military science fiction is an established subgenre with many writers and series in it. Military fantasy, on the one hand, has an acknowledged king. Glen Cook left active duty with the US Navy just a month before the Marine unit he'd been attached to went to Vietnam. His stories are praised especially for the verisimilitude of their military characters, and his long-running *Chronicles of the Black Company* is the premier military fantasy series.[4]

The Black Company is a mercenary band that is elite enough to include wizards, and therefore powerful enough to get tangled up in powers and plots over the company's heads. In the first novel, *The Black Company*, they come to realize they've been hired by an aspiring evil overlord. They are manipulated, one step at a time, into eliminating rival evil powers (imagine they've been hired by Saruman and he's getting them to kill the Nazgûl one bloody step at a time). The battles are tough, and the price paid is high. The soldiers aren't noble warriors declaiming to one another in quatrains on the battlefield, they're real men—men with a hard job to do and the willingness to fight for each other. And as the stakes go up, some of the members of the company start to suspect that a refugee they're sheltering in their midst might just be the child of prophecy who's supposed to rise and overthrow their new boss.

Anthologies

An anthology is a collection of short stories by different authors, generally on a shared theme or in a shared setting. Look, I've had stories in many anthologies. Let me speak a hard truth here: anthologies almost never sell. They can be good for showcasing a new writer. They can be good for doing something collective and themed, like supporting a charity (L.J. Hachmeister's anthology *Instinct*, benefiting animal rescue operations, is a great example). From a writer's perspective, an anthology is an opportunity to network—you get to share space with potentially new writers and work with potentially new editors. From a reader's perspective, an anthology can be a lovely sampler of writers that leads you to find a new favorite (like the soundtrack to the Wim Wenders film *Until the End of the World* introduced me to T-Bone Burnett, Lou Reed, and Nick Cave). But for a publisher . . . I think it's pretty hard to really justify an anthology except as some kind of loss leader.

Light Fantasies

Speculative fiction has long had humorous streaks in it. The late twentieth century saw the launch of a number of humorists who have endured.

Piers Anthony is known for two things. One, he writes a really strong first book for any series he writes, with a significant drop off in wit and energy as a series progresses (compare *Split Infinity* or *On a Pale Horse* to any book following them). And two, he has a humorous fantasy series set in the magical land of Xanth that is, at this writing forty-seven books long.[5] This series is not entirely free of the Piers Anthony Book One Curse—1977's *A Spell for Chameleon* is a more subtle, better book than what follows. But if you can endure puns, broad humor, and the State of Florida reimagined as a fantasy realm, *Xanth* may be for you.

Terry Pratchett's humor was more subtle and sophisticated than Anthony's. It was also directed, satirical, leftist, humanist, and, as his friend Neil Gaiman said, "angry." Although he wrote one-offs, such as the 1990 book *Good Omens* (co-written with Gaiman and televised by Amazon Prime), Pratchett is best known for his forty-one-book series *Discworld*, which over its course satirizes business, politics, religion, sport, cinema, law enforcement, telecommunications, the postal service, and just about everything else.[6]

Robert Lynn Asprin had a varied career. One of his early successes was the creation of Thieves' World, an anthology series of gritty sword and sorcery stories by a wide range of authors in a shared setting (created in 1978) that has gone on to comprise fourteen anthologies, various novels, and multiple tabletop roleplaying incarnations. But Asprin really made his mark as a funny man, with comic military science fiction series *Phule's Company* and, even more, the *Myth Adventures* of journeyman magician Skeeve and scaly green "demon" (short for "dimensional traveler") Aahz. *Myth Adventures* compares favorably to *Xanth* in that both are pun-driven lighthearted adventures, but *Xanth* tends to be more juvenile.[7]

The *Myth Adventures* began with Asprin, then became a joint project of Asprin's together with Jody Lynn Nye, who eventually continued the series herself after Asprin's death. Jody is herself an accomplished humorist of wide range, having her own funny fantasy series about college (*Magic 101*) and fairy godparents (*The Magic Touch*) as well as comic science fiction (*Strong Arm Tactics* and *View from the Imperium*).[8]

We can't talk about humorous speculative fiction and leave out Douglas Adams. Adams was an aspiring TV and radio writer (and sometimes

A Theory of Government

The Well of the Unicorn is a 1948 novel by Fletcher Pratt (first published under the name George U. Fletcher). It tells the tale of Airar Alvarson's attempt to free his homeland from the oppressive Vulkings and is rich with political musings, ultimately warning that, "There is no peace but that interior to us."

actor; he appeared onscreen in two Monty Python sketches) who accidentally become a novelist. *The Hitchhiker's Guide to the Galaxy* started as a radio play, then became a book, then a trilogy, then a trilogy . . . of five books.[9] As if determined to go full circle, the books kept going, becoming an interactive computer game, a TV show, and a movie. Surely the next step for this iconic story of Arthur Dent and his towel, with his friends Ford Prefect and Zaphod Beeblebrox, the two-headed, three-armed former president of the galaxy, is to be broadcast in a radio play.

Chapter Nine

WHEN JAPAN WAS GOING TO TAKE OVER THE WORLD

There was a time when we were unsophisticated about demographics, and didn't realize that if you didn't have babies, you had no future. Japan had been tearing up the economic charts in recent decades by building and selling cheap stuff to the United States, which seemed to work really well. We were so impressed that we started importing Japanese culture. Schoolkids get very excited about martial arts and ninja assassins and yakuza gangsters and giant lizards defending Tokyo from other giant monsters.

Ah, good times.

That was when cyberpunk happened.

The Neuromancer Himself: William Gibson

William Gibson famously and ironically wrote *Neuromancer* on a 1927 Hermes manual portable typewriter.[1] *Neuromancer* was his 1984 debut, a noirish near future crime tale about "lowlifes and high tech." It explored the connections among and boundaries between artificial and human intelligence, military and civilian technology, and physical and electronic space.[2]

Free Range Tech

"One of the things I have taken for granted, in terms of how technology works in the world, is the people that develop it and get it out there don't really know what we are going to do with it until we have really gotten ahold of it and it has become ubiquitous. And then we wind up doing things that its inventors never dreamed of and those things become the real change drivers. That is actually where the whole technocracy thing falls apart for me, because the people who invented it can't predict what we're going to do with it."
—**William Gibson**

In the story, washed-out hacker Henry Case gets recruited for a job. Case's nervous system was deliberately damaged by a former employer, leaving him unable to directly plug into the virtual reality created by the network of interconnected computers Gibson called "cyberspace." He's lured into this new job by the offer of repaired nerves, subject to successful completion of the mission.

The job turns out to be stealing the electronically preserved consciousness of another hacker, but behind that job lie further mysteries and manipulations. Ultimately, Case learns that he's caught up in the machinations of one half of an artificial intelligence, called Wintermute. Created by an ultra-wealthy family, Wintermute is attempting to achieve the next stage of its planned evolution by merging with its other, separately developed half, the "Neuromancer" of the book's title. Wintermute needs Case to complete the final leg of its quest, which involves breaking into an orbital space facility physically as well as hacking its electronic security. Ninjas, ejections into space, and hijinks ensue.

Gibson coined the term "cyberspace," which caught on as a synonym for the internet; *Neuromancer* influenced the vocabulary of technology, though its predictions were not all spot-on. Gibson failed to see the coming importance of the cell phone, famously.

Born Fighting: The Schism of Worldcon One as Taste of Things to Come

How long has fandom been fighting these turf wars over politics and the boundaries of science fiction and fantasy literature? Since the beginning, it turns out. Worldcon One broke down before it started in a split between the "Futurians" and the "Queens Science Fiction Society." The split

> may have been in part over political differences and rival visions for the roles of science fiction (the Futurians were leftist), but interpersonal difficulties over money seem also to have been a factor. The ringleaders of the Futurians were banned from Worldcon One, then showed up at the convention door to protest and hand out pamphlets denouncing the convention's organizers. The ban was upheld and the banned Futurians spent the convention huddling outside, communicating with the rest of the convention by means of unbanned Futurians shuttling in and out. The more things change, it seems, the more they stay the same.[3]

Gibson also didn't invent cyberpunk literature or coin its name. The name was coined as the title of a short story by a writer named Bruce Bethke in 1980 and popularized by the editor Gardner Dozois (see sidebar on p. 76). What "cyberpunk" seems to mean, breaking apart its two components, is stories that involve 1) distributed information technology, i.e., something like the internet, and 2) a rebellious ethos, portraying ragged and underdog characters pushing back against powerful institutions.

Gibson's accomplishment was to achieve popular success, putting a cyberpunk story in front of millions of readers as archetype. This put the genre on the map, paving the way for the making and success of the cyberpunk film *The Matrix* and its sequels. Key motifs carried from *Neuromancer* and its sequels over into the *Matrix* movies include: the central idea that networked computers create a virtual space that a human can access directly by interfacing organically with the machines; a putatively near-future level of technology; deep cynicism about social power structures; ragged, anti-establishment heroes; and a broadly Asian aesthetic encompassing, variously, Asian language-derived slang, samurai, yakuza, ninjas, and martial arts.

The success and persistence of cyberpunk as a literary genre (and as a label!) have led to its appearance in other media, including anime (*Ghost in the Shell*), videogames (*Cyberpunk 2077*), tabletop roleplaying games (*Cyberpunk, Shadowrun*, and others), and even pop music (Billy Idol's *Cyberpunk*).

Ironically, *Neuromancer's* success may also have helped stultify the genre. In other words, its very bigness meant that other stories could only be cyberpunk to the extent that they resembled *Neuromancer*. The mood of *Neuromancer* and its sequels *Count Zero* and *Mona Lisa Overdrive*, for instance, is paranoid-cynical, sweaty-adrenal, west coast-Japanese, so all cyberpunk had to follow suit.

Cyberpunk Parody as Cyberpunk: Neal Stephenson's Snow Crash

Neal Stephenson was arguably more successful than William Gibson in predicting developments in technology in his 1992 cyberpunk novel *Snow Crash*. (Or did he influence the developments?) *Snow Crash* came out at the end of a decade of cyberpunk stories, most famously William Gibson's *Neuromancer* trilogy (above). Cyberpunk novels are gloomy, dystopian affairs in which the heroes are morally gray hackers and mercenaries usually stealing data from secret government or corporate mainframes by hacking into them while the government or corporate enforcers are hunting them down. *Snow Crash* was at the same time the last great cyberpunk novel and also a parody of cyberpunk. For instance, Stephenson's main character, Hiro Protagonist, is a hacker by night, but by day delivers pizzas for the mob. The CIA has become a private, for-profit entity after merger with the Library of Congress. Gated housing developments are sovereign mini-states.

In Stephenson's vision, the Internet has evolved into what he calls the Metaverse. Hackers no longer work directly with code and data streams. Instead, they put on goggles that allow them to see visual representations of the code and the data streams as a place, and as objects they can interact with. Stephenson used the term "avatar" to refer to a user's visual representation in the Metaverse. Hackers' status is influenced by how elaborate and exciting their avatars are.

Stephenson didn't invent the use of the term "avatar" for this purpose. (The word is Sanskrit, and the first use in this sense was in the 1980s computer game *Habitat*.[4]) But the success of *Snow Crash* popularized the term, which is now ubiquitous. More recently, Mark Zuckerberg announced that his next enterprise would be something called "Meta," which would be a visual representation of an unreal space, accessed by users through the Oculus Rift goggles whose technology Facebook had acquired. More than one commentator has observed that Zuckerberg's move was following Stephenson's vision, though, per Stephenson in a March 6, 2023 *Vox* interview, Zuckerberg has never communicated with him about Meta or anything else.

Stephenson was right about virtual reality. How right was he then, or how right will he be, about US dollar hyperinflation, the privatization of the CIA, and the transfer of the powers of government to for-profit corporations?

Science fiction storytelling inspires us to shape technology in exciting directions, and it also warns us what the consequences might be.

★ ★ ★

BaroquePunk

It's not his most famous or bestselling, but my favorite Stephenson books are The Baroque Cycle (published alternatively as eight shortish novels or three huge ones; in either case, the first volume is called *Quicksilver*). The world-spanning adventure takes place in the seventeenth and eighteenth century and involves piracy, counterfeiting, alchemy, the origins of the computer, the development of experimental science, and the birth of modern finance. Attitudinally it is science fiction, exploring connections, e.g., between universal language and artificial intelligence. It has Solomonic gold that weighs more than it should—does this make it fantasy?

Chapter Ten

WITH TOP HAT AND MONOCLE—
THE OTHER PUNKS

A t about the same time that science fiction was pushing for an aesthetic of gray, static-ridden grime, certain strains of fantasy plumped instead for a combination of spats and rayguns.

Victorian Fantasists

At this point King Arthur unexpectedly comes back into our story. Three young friends who were writing students at Cal State Fullerton together and who had corralled Philip K. Dick as a mentor learned that a UK publisher was trying to publish a series of books about the reincarnated Arthur and tried their hands. Their books weren't accepted by that publisher, but two of them published their reincarnated King Arthur novels elsewhere.[1]

K. W. Jeter's *Morlock Night* was a sequel to H. G. Wells's *The Time Machine*. The Morlocks of Wells's novel (the apelike, subterranean posthumans descended from the working class who raise and eat the beautiful surface-dwellers descended from the upper classes, the Eloi) capture the time machine and come back to attack Victorian London. King Arthur returns to fight them off.

In Tim Powers's *The Drawing of the Dark*, an Irish mercenary named Brian Duffy, in Vienna under siege by the forces of Suleiman the Magnificent, is recruited to protect a vat of beer. This beer is the Herzwestern dark, which brews on the bones of the original forgotten culture hero of the west, and which is drawn only once every seven hundred years. At the moment of its drawing, the west is vulnerable to attack, which is why Suleiman is attempting to capture the city. As the action ramps, Duffy learns that he himself is none other than the reincarnated Arthur, whose fate is tied to the drawing of the beer.

On Stranger Tides

The Tim Powers novel that you have probably *seen* is *On Stranger Tides*, which was turned into a Pirates of the Caribbean movie.

By their own account, these three writers championed and drew from Victorian literature at least in part to needle their instructors and fellow students, for whom H. Rider Haggard and Robert Louis Stevenson were passé. They have all gone on to write broader things (and see below).

Powers in particular has become known for his secret histories, in which he gives real-world history with mysterious details a fantastic backstory that explains the oddities. *Declare*, for instance, is a John le Carré–like telling of the story of Kim Philby, the British spy who defected to the Soviet Union, whose plot revolves around the djinn trapped in their ship on Mount Ararat. *The Stress of Her Regard* is the story of a clan of mountain-dwelling vampires who attach themselves to human poets, inspiring them with great visions of beauty while also slowly drinking them dry. The doomed hero of the novel is Lord Byron, and the story includes the summer spent on Lake Geneva with Percy and Mary Shelley and John Polidori, the real-world retreat that birthed *Frankenstein* (see p. 22). Other Powers novels have featured historical writers as protagonists, including *Hide Me Among the Graves* (Dante Gabriel Rossetti) and *My Brother's Keeper* (the Brontë sisters).

Antihero

An antihero is a protagonist who doesn't seek heroic ends or use morally appropriate means. They are common in science fiction and fantasy literature (e.g., Moorcock's Elric, or the various wizards in *The Dying Earth*, or virtually any character in the Thieves' World stories), especially in stories that aim to deconstruct the literature itself or some cultural idea.

What Is Englishness? Susannah Clark's Jonathan Strange and Mr Norrell

Susannah Clark's novel *Jonathan Strange and Mr Norrell* (it looks as if there should be a period in the title; there is not) was published in 2004, several decades after the launch of Jeter, Blaylock, and Powers, by Bloomsbury with its Harry Potter-derived war chest. I want to include it here to make a rough and somewhat disordered arc to show that fantasy literature, though rooted in US publishing, has never lost the interest in England that it got from Dunsany, Tolkien, and Lewis.

Jonathan Strange and Mr Norrell recounts the return of magic to England during the Napoleonic Wars. It poses, at many levels, the question, What does it mean to be English? Her fantasy King of the North, John Uskglass, reminds us that the history of the Windsors and the Tudors and so on is an extremely London-centric, that is to say, *southern* view of England. Geographically, the natural capital of the island was always York. The character of Stephen Black, born a slave but now a perfectly-mannered butler in one of the greatest houses of the land, forces us to consider what allows us to say that a man is an Englishman.

Her two titular wizards duel over the issue of what kind of magic is appropriate for an English magician. Mr. Norrell is an academic. He favors limited access, spells that are carefully controlled and learned strictly form books, and magic practiced only by scholars. Jonathan Strange is an inspired amateur. He comes into his own when he discovers that the stones and trees still abound with wild, intuitive magic, the ancient magic of the King's covenants, the magic of fairies. This is the old magic of the English cunning folk, who learned from and were served by "familiar spirits," but could not exactly clarify, when asked at trial, whether the "familiar spirits" were the spirits of the dead, fairies, angels, or something else altogether.[2] Which of these magicians is more truly English, the Oxford don or the talented hedge wizard? Is it possible that they can both be English, and that these spiritual-intellectual world views can be harmonized?

Fantasy literature explores big, interesting, spiritual questions, questions of meaning and identity.

Dying Earths and Vancian Magic

Dying earth is a speculative fiction genre that imagines Earth in its last gasp, defeated by entropy or about to be swallowed by an engorged sun or otherwise in its final days. Arguably the best dying Earth series is Gene Wolfe's *The Book of the New Sun* (see p. 49). The genre takes its name from *The Dying Earth* and sequels, by Jack Vance. These books are picaresques (meaning, stories that are only loosely connected in an arc), following amoral rogues and magicians back and forth in time as Earth crumbles. Not only did Vance influence Wolfe and give the name to the genre, he also influenced the grandaddy of all tabletop roleplaying games in a fundamental way.

In the early editions of Dungeons & Dragons, magic-users memorized spells between adventures, imprinting them on their memories in their downtime. When a magician cast a spell, he forgot it. This mechanic is taken directly from *The Dying Earth*. The baroque names that D&D spells can have (e.g., *Mordenkainen's Magnificent Mansion* or *Bigby's Clenched Fist*) are also an imitation of and homage to how Vance wrote his wizards in that same series.

Steampunk, the Genre that Never (Yet) Made It

Famously, K. W. Jeter coined the term steampunk in a letter to *Locus Magazine* to describe what he, Blaylock, and Powers were doing (in fact, he called the three of them "steam-punks"[3]). He also described them as writing in "the gonzo-historical manner," a term which I wish had also caught on, since it has broader applicability than "steampunk."

Steampunk is often described as a genre but seems to have more legs as an aesthetic. A book or a movie can be entirely steampunk, or it can be something else, with a steampunk look or steampunk elements. The best definition of the steampunk aesthetic is that it has three elements: technofantasy (the technology in the story is implausible or even built on a known scientific dead end), neo-Victorianism (there is some evocation of or root in the Victorian world), and retrofuturism (there's some connection to the way the artist thinks the past viewed the future).[4]

Jeter's *Morlock Night* is a classic work of steampunk but even more so is his *Infernal Devices*. The protagonist in that novel discovers that his inventor father was more of a genius than he had realized, to the point of building a clockwork twin of his own son, superior to the flesh and blood man in every way. James Blaylock's *Homunculus* (and his other Langdon St. Ives novels) is also classic steampunk. The madcap action is driven by a dirigible possibly containing a tiny space alien circling above London and slowly drifting closer to the ground. Professor Langdon St. Ives competes against the Royal Society, a vivisectionist, a fake evangelist, and others to get to the dirigible first and control its contents.

Tim Powers, who is described as one of the founding fathers of steampunk, never wrote a steampunk novel. The term "gonzo-historical" could indeed describe many of his books, but *The Anubis Gates*, generally pointed to as his seminal steampunk book, has no technology to speak of in it. It's a time travel story about an English professor brought back to 1810 as a tour guide to attend a lecture by Coleridge, who gets caught up

Your Own Private English

Russell Hoban's *Riddley Walker* is a literary post-apocalyptic tale made more challenging by Hoban's use of an invented future English dialect throughout.

in the machinations of Egyptian magicians to overthrow England. It is a tour de force, and it is resolutely a gonzo-historical fantasy novel.

Steampunk gets its share of ribbing (the quote "Steampunk is what happens when goths discover the color brown," attributed to writer Jess Nevins, is harsh but not totally false), and it sometimes functions to add just a touch of brassy color to a novel or movie. Steampunk has had its moments and its influence. Neal Stephenson's novel *The Diamond Age: Or, A Young Lady's Illustrated Primer* is a science fiction novel set in the future, but among a phyle of neo-Victorians who have deliberately adopted the fashions and mores of Victorian England. Its technofantasy consists of nanomachines and matter compilers, but *The Diamond Age* is clearly steampunk, and some of its cover designers have marketed it that way.

What steampunk has never had is a breakout hit, a cultural home-run. Cyberpunk had *Neuromancer* and then *The Matrix*. Steampunk got William Gibson's novel *The Difference Engine* (with Bruce Sterling; a solid novel about the British government's plan to use Charles Babbage's calculating machine for purposes of social control, but not a breakout hit) and Will Smith's *Wild Wild West* (definitely steampunk, and definitely a flop). Steampunk has enough legs that it will come back and try again. Fingers crossed.

Chapter Eleven

EVERYONE BECOMES A CHILD AGAIN

In the twenty-first century, shocking numbers of adults started reading books written for children.

The Boy Who Blew Up: J. K. Rowling's *Harry Potter*

You know what Harry Potter's about, unless you live under a rock, so I won't describe it. Poking around online, you can find a lot of proposals as to what genre the Harry Potter books fall into. They are urban fantasy, contemporary fantasy, high or low fantasy. They are a bildungsroman, they are funny but also tragic. People talking seriously about the genre of Harry Potter almost inevitably miss the point. Harry Potter is literature for children.

Genre, let's remind ourselves, is a bookseller's problem. On which shelf in the bookstore does this book belong? Is it a mystery or a romance? The bookseller has to pick one, and Bob's your uncle, the book goes on a shelf. So a writer for adults is well served to be conscious about what genre she's writing in, and to observe its forms or to break with them deliberately and in the interests of art.

When the target audience is eleven years old, the book goes on the "middle grade" shelf, no matter what's in the book. That means that a writer for children can write a mystery-romance-fantasy-whatever, and as long as the story works, no problem, the book goes on the middle grade shelf. No one says, "I don't know how to sell this book," it just goes right to the kids' section and into the Scholastic catalog.

So people debating seriously the genre of Harry Potter is a symptom of the fact that adults in massive numbers infantilized themselves to read a book for kids, and now have to pretend the book was for grownups all along. I realize that I sound like a curmudgeon, but so be it. I spent too many years riding commuter trains into London and New York City, watching lawyers and investment bankers poring over their dog-eared copies of *Harry Potter and the Exploding Merchandise Machine*, even before publishers accommodated them by producing editions with sober adult covers, to care. If you think Harry Potter are the best books ever, or the best fantasy books ever, I invite you to read more, and grow up.

Dragons Forever: Christopher Paolini's *Eragon*

Christopher Paolini was a teenager when he wrote *Eragon*,[1] and it is a straightforward fantasy novel full of many fantasy tropes. In the full explosion of Pottermania, many readers looking for the next thing to read, but still wanting simple, colorful, child-friendly stories, lit on *Eragon* as the answer. Paolini's models weren't Harry Potter, though, they were the writings of adult SFF writers Mervyn Peake, Ursula K. Le Guin, Frank Herbert, J. R. R. Tolkien, etc., as well as the older sagas and fairy tales those writers were rooted in (his personal recommendation to me was Evangeline Walton's retelling of the medieval Welsh *Mabinogion*; see the sidebar on p. 116). And Paolini, admirably, does the work. Not only is he a conlanger (see sidebar on p. 44), he famously sold the first, self-published edition of *Eragon* by hand, wearing chainmail he himself had made.[2]

Harry Potter's popularity was no doubt a factor in *Eragon*'s success. So was the book's focus on dragons. Dragons have always been a part of fantasy literature (remember, e.g., Smaug in *The Hobbit*). What exactly is fascinating to us about dragons is an interesting question. Let me provide some unscientific data. In January 2023, I was on a panel about dragons at MarsCon in Virginia Beach and it became clear that to some of the panelists, a dragon in a story represented greed. Dragons hoard gold and virgins, neither one of which they have any use for, so they represent the evil will to keep things from others even when you don't benefit yourself. To other panelists, dragons represented freedom. A dragon's power of flight confers unlimited motion and the ability to escape any bond on the dragon's human ally. I called for a show of hands from the audience—who thought dragons represented greed, and who thought they represented freedom. The answer split almost entirely on sex lines. Men said that dragons were greed, and women said that they were freedom.

Now that's super interesting, for many reasons. In the context of this book's subject matter, maybe this tells us why it was a woman, Anne McCaffrey, who devised the famous *Dragonriders of Pern* series, the fantasy novels about elite men and women who ride firebreathing dragons to deal with the dangerous "thread" (which consumes organic matter that it touches) when it falls from the sky. (Except that the novels are really science fiction, because there is no magic as such, and late in the series we learn that the humans are settlers who came to this planet in a spaceship.)[3]

What does this say about *Eragon*? Well, two-bit psychology is worth what you pay for it, but maybe *Eragon*'s combination of classic straight-up Tolkien inspired fantasy together with the female-appealing trope of riding a dragon was a one-two punch that made the book appealing to a wide range of readers and helped lead to the series' massive bestseller status.

And maybe, if you're going to write a fantasy novel, think about having the main character ride a dragon.

Dragonriders

The first published Dragonriders of Pern novel is *Dragonflight*. As with Narnia, you can read these in order of publication or in narrative sequence. As with Narnia, you should read them in order of publication.

Children's Stories Retold: Neil Gaiman's *American Gods*

Rick Riordan writes stories for kids, reinterpreting other people's mythologies (Greek or Norse or Egyptian, etc.) as children's adventure tales. They're quite successful, and outside the scope of this book.

English writer Neil Gaiman is Rick Riordan for grownups. This is not a complete characterization. Some of his books are independent compositions; his children's novel *Coraline* is one of my daughters' favorites, and *Stardust* is a very Dunsany-esque fairytale. But many of his books, and his most famous books, are interpretations of existing mythologies: *Odd and the Frost Giants* (Norse), *Anansi Boys* (West African), *The Graveyard Book* (Kipling), *Bad Omens* and *The Sandman* (Christianity).

"Uncleftish Beholding"

In 1989, Poul Anderson published an essay in *Analog Science Fiction and Fact* explaining atomic theory using only Germanic words, coining new words where necessary.

Maybe the quintessential Gaiman novel is *American Gods*, which tells the story of a convict named Shadow who emerges from prison to find that his expected job has evaporated. He takes work as the bodyguard to a con man who turns out to be Mr. Wednesday (who is the American version of Odin, brought here by his immigrant worshippers); this job leads him into the heart of a war between America's Old Gods (Odin, Ganesha, etc.) and its New Gods (personified forces of modernism like Media). Shadow ultimately comes to believe that the conflict between the gods has been engineered as a kind of sacrifice to Odin. An encounter with a minor serial killer deity at a small town called Lakeside seems to interpret the whole novel by illuminating a horrible co-dependence between gods and mankind. The gods protect mankind, but only at the price of sacrifices. You can forego the sacrifices, but the gods' blessings will fade.

Gaiman is widely read and frequently adapted for movies and TV. In engaging in myth-making and myth-interpreting, he shows us the classic work of fantasy literature. He also shows us one of the risks to the modern artist working with the tools of myth. Because he moves from myth to myth with each new project, and because none of them seem like myths he really believes, he risks feeling glib or shallow, of borrowing the form of fantasy literature but lacking the power thereof.

Peccadillos and Predators

You may be thinking, reading this discussion of "fandom" as a club of (let's be honest, fairly weird) people who regularly get together in hotels to share their esoteric hobbies over long sweaty (I'm looking at you, Dragon Con) weekends, that all of this sounds like a setup in which hanky-panky might ensue. You are not wrong. Hanky panky ensues.

Fandom has a high proportion of folk who are unorthodox in their personal lives. This includes lots of people who are queer or polyamorous. It includes swingers. It includes furries (people who like cosplaying as their cartoon animal alter egos, including sometimes for hookups). It includes Goreans, a lifestyle (for some) or recreational pastime (for others) of female bondage and sexual submission.[4] Most of the people who come to conventions specifically to engage collectively in these activities do so discreetly, furries being the flamboyant exception.

You can see that libertine sexual ethos bleeding back into the novels. Robert Heinlein is an example: early Heinlein work included the juveniles, *Starship Troopers*, and *The Moon Is a Harsh Mistress*, books about competent people facing and solving problems for the species. Later books like *Time Enough for Love* digressed into themes of free love and incest. Similarly, the first Dune novels by Frank Herbert are brilliant examinations of ecological issues in a science fiction setting and a pessimistic, libertarian critique of power. One of the great forces manipulating religious and political power in Dune is the Bene Gesserit witches, with their long-term breeding program and their cynical planting of prophecies they then aim themselves to fulfill. In later Herbert books in the series, we learn that the Bene Gesserit also have sexual superpowers, including the ability to make their genitals vibrate. It's difficult to imagine a more juvenile regression, to be frank with Frank. Terry Goodkind's series *The Sword of Truth* has reputation pithily summarized by a Redditor posting to r/Fantasy, "What's with all the sexual torture in Wizard's First Rule?" Even Patrick Rothfuss seems only to have gotten to the second book of his series before committing himself to philosophical justifications for his own desire to have an open relationship.

Unfortunately, fandom has from time to time generated or sheltered predators. Fantasy author David Eddings and his wife did prison time for keeping an adopted son locked in a cage.[5] In the age before the internet, no one had any incentive to do the hard work of trawling through newspapers or other sources that would have revealed this history, which remained generally unknown until after Eddings died. Marion Zimmer Bradley, regarded as a leading feminist voice in fantasy literature, was accused posthumously by her daughter of sexual molestation and also procuring boys for her husband to molest.[6] Queer Marxist fantasy writer Samuel R. Delany has publicly suggested that people should "expose yourself" to the North American Man/Boy Love Association to "see what it is really about."[7] Most recently, British writer Neil Gaiman's apparently open relationship has led to accusations by two women of rough, non-consensual sex.[8]

An Anti-Narnia: Philip Pullman and *His Dark Materials*

Philip Pullman drew the title *His Dark Materials* as well as the image of the "golden compass" from Milton's *Paradise Lost*, suggesting that he thinks he's engaging in dialog with the Puritan poet. The point of dialog seems to be over the Fall of Man and whether humans, but specifically children, bear any sort of ancestral guilt. I doubt many readers see that connection, because the form Pullman has chosen to use—a fable about children moving across parallel worlds—is much more reminiscent of C. S. Lewis's Narnia stories.

The Golden Compass (*Northern Lights* in the UK) is a steampunk fantasy, set in a fantasy nineteenth-century England in which people travel by coach or dirigible. Though it has been marketed to children, Pullman denies that he wrote it with children in mind. This seems a little disingenuous, since the main characters are children themselves (a writer's rule of thumb, which is *not* ironclad, is that the age of your protagonist is the age of your audience) and the prose is child-friendly. Children in this world are born with dæmons, which are little animal familiars that physically manifest the child's soul. The Church (the "Magisterium") is kidnapping children and experimenting with severing the connection between the children and their dæmons, a process compared to male and female circumcision. The kidnapping of protagonist Lyra Belacqua's friend Roger by the Magisterium sends her on a rescue mission involving an armored polar bear, a cowboy balloonist, and a brigade of flying witches. The mission fails and Lyra's parents sacrifice Roger. Subsequent novels continue the story across different worlds.

Pullman seems to talk about of both sides of his mouth, pretending on the one hand that he doesn't know what the fuss is about, and on the other hand boasting, "My books are about killing God."[9] And in fact, in book three of the series, when the child heroes help God (the "Authority") out of his cage, he is so fragile that he dissolves on the breeze. I think Pullman should fully own it. His books are an attack on belief in God, and also on organized religion.

The answer is not to suppress his books, which won't make the ideas go away. The answer is to be aware of what's in the books, so you know what your children are reading (or watching; this series has been adapted both as a movie and as a streaming series), and to answer them with other books.

Chapter Twelve

VAMPIRES AND OTHER DARK TALES

Historically, stories about vampires serve the same function as murder ballads like *Pretty Polly*. The vampire story told over the campfire is a warning to the young women of the tribe, that strange men who invite them to come away to exotic places seem alluring, but can be violent predators. In recent years, that reading has been turned on its head. What do we make of women writers exalting the sexual attractiveness of vampires? Is this a male/female dichotomy like the understanding of dragons seem to be? Was there always a whispered women's wisdom that said, "Yes, but sometimes the strange man is the right one"? Is it a manifestation of the pro-choice mentality—it's the protagonist's body, she can choose to sacrifice it to the vampire if she wants?

I don't know, but it has certainly sold a lot of books.

Vampires in Louisiana: Anne Rice and Charlaine Harris

Anne Rice was raised Catholic but became agnostic as a young woman. As an agnostic, she wrote *Interview with the Vampire* and sequels, very popular erotic vampire novels. Following a return to Catholicism in her sixties,[1] she wrote two novelizations of the early life of Jesus (the proposed third and fourth volumes did not materialize). In her seventies, she apparently saw herself as a secular humanist, though without explaining what she understood by that.

Interview with the Vampire is the interview of a two-hundred-year-old vampire New Orleans Louis by an unnamed reporter. The central thread running through Louis's story is his relationship and conflict with Lestat, the vampire who turned him to vampirism. He unwillingly makes his own protégé vampires and is introduced to larger vampire society, which leaves him sickened and appalled. Eventually Louis drives away the reporter, who wants to be turned into a vampire himself.

Interview is not superficially erotic even to the extent of Bram Stoker's *Dracula*. Presumably because it chronicles eros-like relationships among male vampires, it and its sequels gained a devoted LGBTQ following. Charlaine Harris's *Southern Vampire Mysteries*, by contrast, contain explicit sex. The narrator is a living woman and telepath, and her adventures involve various passionate relationships, sex clubs, and other hijinks.

The positive revaluation of vampire eroticism has extended into stories about those who slay vampires. Laurell K. Hamilton's *Anita Blake: Vampire Hunter* books (thirty and counting) chronicle a wide range of sexual adventures of its necromancer protagonist, including notably in *Narcissus in Chains*, in which she gains a sexual superpower from a vampire lover that gives her great power but requires her to have sex multiple times a day to keep the power under control.

Vampires Who Get Married and Have Children: Stephenie Meyer's *Twilight*

Perhaps the ironic apotheosis of stories that see vampire lovers as a positive is *Twilight*. You know what this book is about, I'm not going to describe it. I will offer the following comment. For good or ill, Edward is a vision of *domesticated* vampire eros. He doesn't just want to drink

A Whole Other Book?

The Icelandic translation of Bram Stoker's *Dracula*, *Makt Myrkranna* ("Powers of Darkness"), differs so much from *Dracula* that it is thought to be either a translation from a lost first draft of the book or (I think more likely) simply the creative work of the "translator." It was panned on release in 1901.

Bella's blood (he tells her that her blood smells absolutely and uniquely fascinating to him, and that this is the basis of his attraction to her), he wants a committed relationship. Indeed, ultimately he wants to have children with her. This is how Bella squares the circle for the reader who wants her to be romantically with both vampire Edward and werewolf Jacob. Laurell K. Hamilton would have had them in a polyamorous relationship; Stephenie Meyer has Edward and Bella have a daughter, who grows up at a magically accelerated rate so she can marry Jacob.

Stephenie Meyer wants to have her cake and eat it, too. She wants to embrace powerful vampire eroticism, and she wants that eros to then domesticate itself into a bourgeois marriage.

Dystopias Come Back into Fashion: Suzanne Collins and her Imitators

The striking thing about the dystopian fiction craze in the early twenty-first century is that it manifested as young adult literature. Does this tell us that young people in the early years of the twenty-first century were especially open to the message that the future might be dark? Or does it tell us that the adults who were open to those ideas were also reading at a young-adult level?

I judge a "good" dystopia to be one that warns its readers of a real threat or tendency in society. Both *Nineteen Eighty-four* and *Brave New World* are good dystopias. *Nineteen Eighty-four* warns about the totalitarian political tendency to control people by controlling news and history. *Brave New World* warns against building social classes around the intelligence of participants. These both anticipated real (and now pressing) social problems in the West. *The Handmaid's Tale*, by sad contrast, wants to pretend that some group of Bible believers intends to coopt the wombs of women and force them to reproduce. This is silly nonsense.

The Excommunication of Mercedes Lackey

Author Mercedes Lackey is an old-style writer who came up in fandom. She was a fan in fandom and a filk songstress who then made good by becoming a published writer and then made better by prolifically producing well-loved novels, over 140 as of this writing. She has published traditionally but at the pace of the most frenetic of the self-publishers. Her Valdemar setting is a fan favorite and, on a personal note, her Herald Mage trilogy in that setting was the first series I ever read with a gay protagonist. Indeed, Mercedes has long been a socially progressive voice in SFF literature. In my personal experience, Mercedes and her husband (writer and artist) Larry Dixon have also been extremely generous, welcoming, and decent people.

In 2022, the Science Fiction and Fantasy Writers Association (SFWA) announced that it was making Mercedes a Grand Master. This was a merited honorific in light of her career. In light of the generally quite progressive politics of SFWA, it was also unsurprising—Mercedes in her writing had helped paved the way for today's progressive writers working with issues of gender. This made what happened next appalling.

Mercedes was naturally a guest of honor at the Nebula Conference, the conference at which she was being awarded with Grand Master status. The conference was, of course, virtual, being conducted over Zoom or some similar platform. While on a panel called "Romancing Sci Fi & Fantasy," Mercedes referred to her friend Samuel R. Delany as "a colored writer." Mercedes was at the time a seventy-two-year-old woman, and might have been forgiven for not realizing that the preferred euphemism had become "writer of color." A third-rate nobody complained. Mercedes and Larry were digitally locked out of the conference. They weren't informed and they weren't given an opportunity to respond. SFWA released a statement that Mercedes had "used a racial slur," which must certainly have made people hearing about this for the first time from the press release assume she had said something other, and worse, than "colored."[2]

Mercedes Lackey was kicked out of her own career-crowning celebration by woke, ax-grinding, language cops.

Mercedes, no doubt stunned and wounded by an attack from her own people, issued an apology on Tumblr saying that she had misspoken. This should have been obvious from the start. Samuel Delany indicated that he had taken no offense.[3] This was an obviously rational response. SFWA has never apologized. The third-rate nobody never apologized.

I will paraphrase the philosopher Nicholas Edward Cave. Step One: Go out to eat with the cannibals. Step Two:

Dystopias are nothing new. The breakthrough novel in the recent flowering was Suzanne Collins's *The Hunger Games*, which is considerably more accomplished as literature than most of its imitators, and also a better dystopia. In the novel, a future America is divided into thirteen districts and the Capitol. Every year, two youths are chosen by lottery as "tributes" from each district and entered in a contest that is a battle to the death. When the protagonist Katniss's younger sister is chosen as tribute, Katniss volunteers to take her place. Fighting for her life, she finds herself a hero to her impoverished district and then to all the districts who groan under the oppressive yoke of the Capitol.

The Hunger Games shows us a society in which mass media entertainment, the desire for celebrity, and division into warring groups are used by the governing class in the decadent national capital to keep the population under control and remain in power. It also strikes a note on children and violence. The tributes are all over the age of twelve but still youths (making them the age of the intended audience, "young adults"). This means that in the book (and in the movie adaptation), children kill each other. This ought to horrify the readers and the filmgoers, referencing young gangsters in the US as well as child soldiers in third world countries—as of this writing, recent news stories claim that children are being trained by gangs in Sweden to carry out lethal hits because they are too young to be prosecuted.[4] If you've read or seen *The Hunger*

Games, I'll let you decide for yourself to what extent the story conveyed the evil of forcing children to commit acts of violence, and to what extent that was offset or undercut by the glamor of children committing acts of heroism.

Other dystopias offered in recent years include: a society in which equality is achieved by making everyone and everything the same (*The Giver*), a society which controls all personal decisions, including romantic decisions (*Matched*), a society in which everyone is sorted into factions by a personality test (*Divergent*), and a society in which the young as used as test subjects for vaccines for a civilization-threatening disease (*The Maze Runner*). I'll let you judge which of these diagnose real threats to society and which describe perils that only exist in the authors' minds.

Literary Apocalypse

A Canticle for Leibowitz, by Walter M. Miller Jr. is a post-apocalyptic tale of monks carrying the seed of civilization through a future collapse. It is enlivened by the humorous misinterpretation of a shopping list.

Climate Dystopias

The always-pending environmental disasters that have been a staple of mainstream news my entire life have infiltrated speculative fiction as well. A notable example is Paolo Bacigalupi's *The Windup Girl*, sometimes characterized as a "biopunk" novel. The ostensible main plot revolves around a genetically engineered sex slave named Emiko and her Pinocchio-esque desire to become a real girl by finding others of her kind. The real story is about the AgriGen Corporation's oppressive campaign to dominate global farming with their genetically engineered seeds, and their efforts to find the hidden seedbank that has allowed Thailand to resist economic enslavement. The real heroes of the story are the Thai leaders who overthrow their own government and drive out AgriGen. This is certainly science fiction. It's also essentially political pornography, no more believable than Roland Emmerich's self-indulgent 2004 film *The Day After Tomorrow*, which tried to make us all believe in the doomsdays that Al Gore was preaching.

Chapter Thirteen

POST-CYBERPUNK SCIENCE FICTION

Cyberpunk was a wave of dark science fiction, cynical and nihilistic. You can see that spirit in the movies, manifesting as a slew of grungy, pessimistic films: *Alien* (1979), *Bladerunner* (1982), *Terminator* (1984), *Robocop* (1987), *Predator* (1987), *Total Recall* (1990), *Gattaca* (1997), and *Minority Report* (2002), to name just a few. But science fiction had to be more than just pessimism if it was to survive.

Losing Your Humanity to Save Mankind: Orson Scott Card

Orson Scott Card has written for many mediums and about many subjects, in the genres of science fiction and fantasy and outside the genres. He has also taught literature and writing and has published other writers, making him an influential and popular writer.[1]

But he's known above all, to the average reader, for one book. That doesn't mean that his other works are inferior. It just means that *Ender's Game* has proven enduringly popular, and a perennial classic. Like philosopher David Hume, Card wrote his masterpiece (or at least, his most popular work) right out of the gate.

Ender's Game is a big idea book. Earth faces an existential threat from an insect-like species with a hive mind. Earth's Battle School recruits

American Fantasy

For a taste of Card's fantasy writing, check out *Seventh Son*, the first of his Alvin Maker series. This is fantasy set in nineteenth century alternate frontier America, which inspired, among other things, my own, more epic-scaled, *Witchy Eye*.

and trains young Andrew "Ender" Wiggin because Ender, who is small, acts pre-emptively and ultra-violently to win battles that he knows he will lose otherwise. This is behavior he learned to defend himself from his sociopath brother. The fact that boys he is fighting die from their injuries is concealed from him. Ender trains at computer simulated battles, commanding fighter pilots. At the end of one battle, he sacrifices his entire fleet but achieves a win that defeats the entire enemy fleet. At this point he's informed that the simulation was real, and Ender was commanding the human defense forces remotely.

So far as that goes, we have a classic science fiction story. How can humans win against such an overwhelming enemy? The humans must create a human leader who can fight like a hivemind himself, fighting ruthlessly to protect the collective, even at the cost of all the fighting individuals. Even at the cost of that one human's soul.

Where Card takes Ender's story to the next level is over the rest of the series. Ender takes on the persona of a "Speaker for the Dead," seeking reconciliation. In this role, he comes to tell not just the story of *The Hive Queen*, but also the story of his sociopath brother, who has become *The Hegemon*.

Not Everyone Will Like the Inevitably Socialist Future: Iain M. Banks

Iain M. Banks's *Culture* series explores the ramification of a far-future, post-scarcity civilization. Advanced AIs run the Culture, and not only is food never at a shortage, nothing else is either. Culture members spend all their times finding ways to entertain themselves, which for many of them seems to be changing back and forth from one sex to the other over time. Obviously, this is a vision of the future that is economically and socially left, and committed to the plasticity of human nature. As such, frankly, it's not very interesting. No scarcity means no hard choice, so we're basically imagining away problems. No problems means no plot and no stories, everyone just gets what they want, starting right away at the happily ever after. The end.

To get a story, Banks has to tell a truth: even if we could have no scarcity at all, some people would choose not to take the deal. If offered Banks's idea of heaven, some people would resist. So the novels take place at the edges of the Culture, where some person or group decides they won't go along, because they have religious objections, or they can't accept egalitarianism because they themselves wish to rule, or because they want revenge, or they are chauvinistic for some other reason.

All of which tells us that scarcity and the tragic nature of human existence are a good reason to reject socialism. But if you take them away, there will still be reasons not to accept a collective. Banks might not think the reasons are good ones, but he knows they exist.

Child of a Famous Father: Lois McMaster Bujold

Lois McMaster Bujold's father was a famous engineer, and she has commented more than once on the challenges of growing up with a famous father. Like any good artist, she has worked those feelings and that struggle of her own into her books, in the form of Miles Vorkosigan.[2]

The Vorkosigan Saga takes place in a galaxy where the only known sentient inhabitants are humans. At least two interstellar empires exist, but most planets have their own government, of various sorts. Miles is the son of aristocratic parents, the Count and Countess of Vorkosigan, who was poisoned in utero as part of an assassination attempt on his father. His grandfather, believing the child will be unfit to be a Count, tries to murder him in the artificial womb, but is thwarted. The lasting effects on Miles are fragile bones, leaving him short and hunch-backed, with an absolute necessity to make his way by brains rather than by brawn. Over some eighteen novels plus short stories, Miles founds and leads a mercenary company and has a long career as an undercover agent, with a healthy heaping of diplomat and detective on the side, and engages in sundry romances. Miles is razor smart with a particular gift for improvised tactics, but he also succeeds by indomitable energy and a refusal to take no for an answer.

The combination of brilliance, high energy, and fragility create an interesting image. Miles engages in rigorous sports such as swimming and horseback riding, even though it can result in broken bones for him. Given the neo-feudal setup of the Vorkosiverse, maybe Bujold is showing us in the character of Miles what is needed in the aristocrats of the future, the aristocrats of outer space. A person of that energy and brilliance, despite all the wounds, might also live up to a famous father.

Celtic Fantasy

Celtic tales have cast a long shadow in fantasy, with and without King Arthur attached. The medieval collection of Welsh folktales, *The Mabinogion*, has been retold straight by Evangeline Walton and cut down and remixed for children by Lloyd Alexander as *The Chronicles of Prydain*.

Welsh and Cornish folklore also made it into Susan Cooper's The Dark Is Rising Sequence, five truly excellent young adult fantasy books about the Light, a magico-spiritual force protecting and guiding Britain through a time of attack by the Dark. One of the heroes of the series is a son of King Arthur who was protected from the forces that killed Arthur by hiding him in the future.

Mary Stewart was a writer of romance mysteries who saw the rising popularity of Arthurian tales and jumped genres to write *The Crystal Cave, The Hollow Hills*, and *The Last Enchantment*. This is the story of Arthur told from the point of view of the wizard Merlin, or rather Myrddin, who is the son of a Welsh princess.

Though not expressly Celtic in setting, Patricia McKillip's Riddle Master trilogy deserves mention here. Its Celtic-inspired names, its lyricism, and its choice of riddle-speakers and harpists as its main characters make it fit right in with the medieval Welsh tales of Taliesin.

Animals Are People Too: David Brin

David Brin is a hard science fiction writer from California whose most famous books (three standalone novels and a trilogy) take place in what is sometimes called the "Uplift Universe," named, interestingly, for a technological idea rather than for a character or a plot. The core idea of the setting is that in the multi-galactic civilization of the stories, a "patron" species will deliberately undertake to modify a pre-sentient "client" species until the client species becomes sentient, that is to say, uplifted. The newly uplifted species then owes its patron a long period of indenture.

Brin coined the term "uplift" to describe deliberately shaping the development of a species toward sentience. This word has since been adopted in other fiction, game settings, and even scientific literature.

The process of uplift is thought to have begun two billion years ago with a mysterious vanished species called the Progenitors. Humans, interestingly, have no known patron, believing themselves to have been produced by true biological evolution. This belief has made enemies for the humans of most sentient species in the galaxy; in the meantime, humans had already uplifted dolphins and chimps before they ran into other sentients.

The concept of uplift drives the core themes of the stories, which revolve around ideas of colonialism, speciesism, and religious rejection of the novel. Uplift is presented as a positive enterprise. This might be seen in contrast with the author's judgments on the technological creation of a sentient man in *Frankenstein* or Doctor Moreau's human-animal hybrids in the H. G. Wells novel that bears his name.

The Galactic Canterbury Tales: Dan Simmons

Hyperion is one of the masterworks of science fiction. If you were to set out to try to read a top ten of the genre, or even, say, a top three . . . you'd probably have to choose *Dune*, *Ender's Game*, and *Hyperion*. Of the three, *Hyperion* is the one that is self-consciously literary.

A planet at the edge of civilization, Hyperion, beyond the reach of the teleportation gates that connect inhabited worlds, contains a monument called the Time Tombs. The Time Tombs are a novelty because they are traveling backward in time. They are protected by a creature called the Shrike. On the eve of Hyperion's conquest by hostile powers, a final expedition travels to the Time Tombs.

Those on the expedition are pilgrims, traveling to the Time Tombs because they want something. On the journey, they take turns telling each other their tales. Each pilgrim's tale provides a compelling reason for that pilgrim to have made the journey, despite the massive risks involved. The stories weave together to create a cohesive novel, and then end abruptly, when the characters approach the Time Tombs and the Tombs begin to glow.

Medieval Christianity—Katherine Kurtz

Given how much fantasy tends to wear the skin and clothing of medieval Europe, it's not surprising that from time to time a fantasy series would embrace the religion of medieval Europe as well. One great example is Katherine Kurtz's Chronicles of the Deryni, which are set in Gwynedd, a fantasy analog to England in a fantasy analog to Europe. The series chronicles the difficulty that two almost-identical human races have living together, when one is magically-talented and the other is not. It includes priests and nuns as characters, disputes over whether astonishing events are magical in nature or acts of God, real Latin, and quotes from the Bible.

In the way that *Dune* explores power and ecology, and *Ender's Game* explores questions of the individual verses the collective, *Hyperion* explores time and its corollaries: loss and memory, commitment and betrayal, decay and rebirth, beauty and art. You reach the end feeling like you've resolved many mysteries, and had an encounter with Time.

Napoleonic Warships in Space: David Weber

I had a fan of David Weber's inquire about what projects Weber was working on once. I told him what I knew and the fan said, "You know, it's pretty clear that David wants to write an actual Napoleonic naval novel. Tell him he should go ahead and do it. I'd read it!"

The fan was making reference to Weber's *Honor Harrington* series, which is unabashedly Napoleonic naval fiction in space. The main series now contains fifteen novels, with as many novels in spinoff series as well as a number of anthologies and a series companion. The central figure is Honor Harrington, and Weber treats her just like C. S. Forrester treated Horatio Hornblower (whose initials she shares) or Patrick O'Brian treated Jack Aubrey. We meet her as Commander Honor Harrington of the Royal Manticoran Navy, early in her career and with a small command, and follow her exploits and promotions. As of the fifteenth novel, *Uncompromising Honor*, she is Admiral of the Grand Fleet. Weber has suggested that Honor will die at the end of her career, but he's already pushed that back a couple of times. Either she hasn't reached the end of her career, or he doesn't have the heart to do it. Both may be true.

In the first book, *On Basilisk Station*, Honor commands a light cruiser in a remote outpost that has been treated as a dumping grounds for officers who are currently in disfavor. She has rowdy officers and a ship that has been stripped of most of its standard complement of weaponry, but she's in a system where nothing is expected to happen. Naturally, things happen. Honor has to whip her officers into shape and get creative with her weaponry resources to deal with what appears at first to be drug smuggling, but then turns out to be an invasion plan.

You can imagine all of this happening with wooden three-masters

Military SF Romance

For an unconventional take on military science fiction—romance novels, in which the action-hero burden is carried by the romantic-interest male character—check out Dorothy Grant's *Going Ballistic*.

in a remote island chain in the Indian Ocean. That's good; David has updated a genre with many fans. He is unironic with the material thematically, telling stories of duty, courage, hard work, and sacrifice in the line of duty.

And I personally think Honor Harrington is going to live forever.

Chapter Fourteen

URBAN FANTASY, WITH AND WITHOUT CITIES

Urban Fantasy can be something of an elastic term. As noted above, it has been applied to Harry Potter, though the Potter stories mostly take place in a boarding school in the English countryside. As discussed below, more than one popular urban fantasy writer's books tend to take place in remote corners of America, and are only ever urban by accident. So urban fantasy seems to be a label that really means "contemporary fantasy," in other words, fantasy novels that might contain a car or a gun.

Slumming It: Mainstream Literary Writers and SFF

From time to time, a literary novelist produces a science fiction or fantasy novel. The classic move when doing this is to deny that the novel is SFF or speculative fiction. This has been true most notably of dystopian novels, like Margaret Atwood's *The Handmaid's Tale* or P. D. James's *The Children of Men*. It's true of novels with fantastical elements, too, such as Haruki Murakami's *The Wind-Up Bird Chronicle*, whose partisans might say that the "magical elements are not meant to be fantasy: they are meant to be a deeper level of our true reality."[1] It's true of much of the work of Michael Chabon, whose best stuff is or flirts heavily with being alternate history, superhero, and sword and sandal. Maybe in this book we've seen enough reason for those literary writers and readers to try to avoid the perceived taint of speculative fiction: SFF is pulp literature, it is aimed at the masses, it's an intramural nerd art form developed by and for fandom, it's associated with weirdos (I say this with affection for weirdos, of which I am one).

The Boundary with Paranormal Romance: Sherrilyn Kenyon

Where urban fantasy is written for a female audience, it also bleeds into a genre called "paranormal romance." Where exactly the line between the two lies is probably in the eye of the bookseller and consumer. An urban fantasy novel can feature a great deal of romance, as well as werewolves and vampires, but at some point, the book becomes a romance novel that happens to feature werewolves and vampires. This is not a problem or genre confusion, it just reminds us that genre is an abstraction for talking about books, and not an absolute, Platonic set of categories that exists in reality. My stab at a rule of thumb would be that if you're trying to interest male readers in a book, you can call it YA or urban fantasy, but don't call it paranormal romance.

A writer whose work gets both labels is Sherrilyn Kenyon. Kenyon is massively successful, with a huge following, most of whom are women. (I should also say that, in my personal experience, she's a tremendously kind and generous person.) Her interlocking "hunters" series in her dark-hunter universe exist in a Greek myth-inspired Earth rich with shape-shifters, fallen gods, and demons. Her stories feature a lot of romance, including romance of the . . . explicit . . . variety. Sometimes these books get called urban fantasy. (The prequel *Chronicles of Nick* are YA.) They certainly do feature gods and monsters, and they comprise a sprawling, many-book series in a persistent universe, just as Terry Brooks's Shannara books do. I think her audience is mainly women and I think the romance in the books is primary, which I think is reflected in the books generally being called "paranormal romance."

Were-Coyote: Patricia Briggs

Patricia Briggs's Mercedes "Mercy" Thompson lives in the tri-cities of Washington. If you're not familiar, these are three closely linked small cities in the eastern part of the state and on the Oregon border. These are high altitude, arid places, with a lot of agriculture and a fair share of wilderness.

So . . . "urban" fantasy.

Briggs's most famous character is mechanic Mercy Thompson, whose father was a Blackfoot bull rider who died before she was born. From him, she inherited the gift of being able to change shape into a coyote at will, along with some supernaturally sharp senses. Men interacting with bulls and humans changing shape into animals put us squarely into the space of the old cave paintings. In the first book, *Moon Called*, Mercy gives a job to a teenage drifter who she knows is a werewolf. When heavies from a laboratory turn up looking for their escaped werewolf, and Mercy kills one of the heavies—also a werewolf—things get complicated.

There's plenty of romance in the books (in *Moon Called*, two werewolves both get interested in Mercy, which drives territorial pack infighting). Some readers have expressed displeasure in reviews about the increasing prominence of relationship themes over the course of the series. On balance, though, and acknowledging that this is not science but a subjective scale, it feels like Mercy Thompson is urban fantasy.

Mythic Arizona

One of the earliest urban fantasy novels was Charles Finney's *The Circus of Dr. Lao* (1935), in which a traveling circus exhibits mythical creatures in small-town Arizona.

Wizard P.I.: Jim Butcher's *Dresden Files*

Jim Butcher's wizard Harry Dresden is definitely urban. He's a private investigator in Chicago. On the other hand, his magical talent causes more complex technologies to malfunction, so he drives a Volkswagen Bug and, when he uses a gun, it's a revolver. Butcher apparently wanted to write epic fantasy but was encouraged in a writing class to write something like Laurell K. Hamilton's *Anita Blake: Vampire Hunter.* So in this spectrum that runs from sex with monsters at one end to blowing up monsters with nuclear bombs (see below) at the other, maybe we should think of Harry Dresden as paranormal romance for men.

Maybe it's because of his stated preference for epic fantasy, or maybe it's implicit in his choice to lean into hard-boiled and noir elements in the storytelling, but there's a feeling of amusement that runs through the Dresden stories, as if Butcher himself can't quite take them seriously. Dresden bribes fairies for their help with pizza. After a hard night battling sorcerers and demons, he joins his tabletop roleplaying group to play a mindless barbarian. He's assisted by Bob, a lecherous demon trapped in a skull that can't get enough of slutty romance novels (nod to Dresden's own proximity to paranormal romance?).

In book seven of the series, *Dead Beat*, Dresden uses necromancy to reanimate the skeleton of a tyrannosaurus in a museum (the tyrannosaurus is named Sue). His ally controls the dinosaur bones with polka music, played on an accordion. This is a scene so over-the-top comical in both its premise and its execution that it would have killed almost any series that included it. Harry Dresden jumped the shark (a reference to the *Happy Days* episode in which the Fonz jumps over a shark on waterskis, meaning that the series went too far to be able to come back, and became irredeemable). Except that fans took the necromantic dinosaur scene in stride and kept reading. I think readers were able to accept Sue the polka-dancing tyrannosaurus because the truth is that the books never took themselves seriously in the first place. The Harry Dresden stories are something of a spoof on paranormal romance and urban fantasy. This may also be why, though Harry does get seduced and abused by various femme fatale fairies and vampiresses, the woman with whom he has an enduring relationship is a stubbornly non-paranormal cop.

Urban Fantasy in Rural Alabama, with Guns: Larry Correia's *Monster Hunter International*

Larry Correia's debut, *Monster Hunter International*, famously opens with a guy, Owen Pitt, killing his boss by throwing him out the office window. But only after the boss turns into a werewolf. Pitt is an accountant, but also burly and muscular and a serious gun aficionado, and his successful boss-defenestration brings him to the attention of an elite private contractor to the federal government, MHI.

There's an aesthetic of awesomeness that runs through the MHI novels. By this I mean that the question, "Wouldn't it be awesome if . . . ?" seems to be the core driver to how Correia builds tales. His protagonist in this, his flagship series, is modeled on Correia himself (Correia is a career accountant and a former gun store owner, and a large man). That doesn't make this Gary Stu fiction. Pitt doesn't have his problems magically solved for him and isn't amazingly good at everything he touches. But the kernel of the stories seems to be Correia imagining, "What would be fun?" and then writing that. Correia himself is obviously entertained, and the result is that the books engage the reader.

In the *Monster Hunter International* stories, monsters are real. Yes, the monsters you know about, and they basically work the way you expect them to. This includes vampires and werewolves, etc., but also orcs and elves. Where there are twists, they are always comical twists in the direction of fun, though Correia plays them with a straight face. His elves live in trailer parks and look like children. His orcs pilot helicopters. Some of the monsters are trouble for the (mostly oblivious) human

Manly Stories

Manly Wade Wellman wrote two early series of what would be today classified as urban fantasy:

- John Thunstone is an occult detective whose first appearance is in "The Third Cry to Legba."
- Silver John the Balladeer is a Korean War veteran and folksinger who fights evil with his silver-stringed guitar and whose first appearance in a novel is in *The Old Gods Waken*.

population, so the federal government deals with them by putting bounties on the monsters. MHI hunts monsters for the bounties, generally (not always) finding them out in rural and wilderness areas, where they can more easily hide.

There are romantic relationships in these books, but they are definitely subplots. These are stories about operators, ex-soldiers and law enforcement who put their lives on the line to protect humanity from the things that go bump in the night. The books have a rugged, masculine streak of independence about them—the feds, if they show up, usually add red tape and complicate the situation. The heroes are the men and women getting the job done, and doing it with big guns.

Chapter Fifteen

THE TWO GREAT DEVIANCIES OF MODERN FANTASY

It matters what literature is for. At the fringes, any literature will generate the philosophically light variants that only seek to entertain. There's nothing wrong with that. A novel that lightens a reader's stress by letting him immerse himself in an imaginary world of elves and chainmail for an hour is a worthy thing.

But fundamentally, any book that seeks only to entertain is a kind of porn. That's probably too harsh a judgment, I don't mean to say that literature that does nothing more than entertain brings the same kinds of social ills that actual pornography does. But purely entertaining books are ephemeral, bubblegum, they have no meaning, they add nothing to the reader's soul.

I don't mean that every book needs to be a ponderous, theme-heavy exploration of ethics or metaphysics. But if fantasy gets too far away from the core of what makes it really valuable, it loses its power. It risks becoming pointless, unnecessary, unimportant, trivial, the mere fetish of a subculture rather than the noble quest to illuminate the human condition.

In recent years, two trends have dragged fantasy away from its core. One of these is technical (meaning, a matter of storytelling technique) and the other is philosophical. I won't name very many names here. If you're in the literature, you can see for yourself who I'm talking about. And I think that both these trends are approaching their eventual end, and it's about time.

Hard Magic Is the Fan Fiction of Gaming

There have probably always been writers who have wanted to devise their own artificial "magic systems," i.e. construct imaginary ways for magic to work in the writers' imaginary worlds. In a sense, the roots of hard magic lie in actual magic, and the idea that the universe works according to rules that are knowable but generally unknown, and that a person can learn those rules and cause effects in the world. For instance, Ursula Le Guin incorporated real-world ideas about how knowing the secret names of a thing or a person would give the magician power over that thing or person into *A Wizard of Earthsea*.

But a funny thing happened to fantasy literature. It got popular. It got made into movies, and it got made into games. And if you are going to design a game in which a player can participate in the role of a wizard (in classic *Dungeons & Dragons*, a "magic-user"), then you need rules to define how that works. In the same way that you have rules that define which weapons your "fighter" knows how to use, and which dice to roll against which target numbers to determine the effect when he swings a sword, you need rules to determine which magical effects your magic-user is capable of achieving, and what he needs to have to achieve them, and which dice to roll against which target numbers. And for the purposes of game fairness, usually these systems need to be balanced, so the fighter doesn't feel ripped off because the magic-user can do all kinds of crazy stuff and the fighter just swings his sword.

A tabletop roleplaying game needs a "combat system" for deciding combat outcomes in the game and a "magic system" for deciding the outcomes of magic. You sometimes see this explicitly, as in the game

Rolemaster, which published its combat system in a book called *Arms Law* and its magic system in a book called *Spell Law*.

A tabletop roleplaying game can be reasonably sophisticated about its artificial magic because the game mechanics exist in a narrative universe created by the players, in which theoretically anything can happen. Such a magic system still exists in a story, and the story can be driven by analogy, wonder, and myth.

Tabletop Gaming: From the Satanic Panic to Big Screen

Nothing so neatly captures the way my personal culture has inverted over the last forty years as the odyssey made by tabletop roleplaying games (TTRPGs). A TTRPG is Dungeons & Dragons, or a game played in the same fashion as Dungeons & Dragons. Players sit around a table, imagining they are characters in a science fiction or fantasy setting. One player presents a series of challenges to the other in narrative form ("You see a band of orcs attacking the village. What do you do?") and the others cooperate to overcome those challenges. A gaming group with resources may have painted miniatures and miniature landscapes, musical soundtracks, and tricked-out gaming tables. In my youth, we made do with pencil and paper, a set of shared dice, and a bag of Twizzlers.

TTRPGs are said to have evolved from wargames, which are said to have come from miniature military simulations held to train Prussian officers, refereed by experienced sergeants. By the 1980s, when the hobby was denounced as Satanic and ludicrously connected with occultism and teen suicide, the wargame aspect generally had taken a backseat to something that looked more like a quest. Players didn't fight each other with armies (generally), they cooperated to rescue princesses and retrieve lost treasures. They (we) were collectively creating the same kinds of fantasy (and science fiction) narratives we loved to read in books. For many of us, that was a furtive activity engaged in late at night at sleepovers and not approved by everyone's parents.

How the worm has turned! Somehow (again, maybe it was that nerds took over Silicon Valley and then the culture), the outlaw hobby of my childhood is now on the big screen, with D&D movies (good, big-budget movies) but also series such as *Stranger Things*. Where once a good gaming session might have been three hours at the park and no one's character sheet blew away, now Hollywood stars like Joe Manganiello and Henry Cavill openly show their elaborate gaming rooms and talk about their TTRPG campaigns.

When tabletop roleplaying simplifies down into a more structured game, say a card game like *Magic: the Gathering*, the magic system has to become more inflexible, mechanical, and rules-driven. Wonder and improvisions and surprise are chased out, replaced by the mechanical decisions of which card to play and how many tokens are necessary to flip over the opponent's card or take it into one's own hand.

Starting earlier but really gaining steam in the 2010s, hard magic blew up in fantasy literature. There were and are other writers, but the Smaug of this Lonely Mountain is Brandon Sanderson. He himself has said that a story's magic only needs to be "hard" to the extent that the detail of how the magic works is essential to the resolution of the story. However, since he heavily favors hard magic himself, his off-the-charts popularity has distorted the perception of many readers and writers, causing them to think that hard magic is somehow core to fantasy literature. In fact, the opposite is true.

Hard magic is the imposition of game logic on magic in stories. Wonder and analogy and myth are stripped out in favor of pseudo-scientific constructs that give the illusion of being solidly engineered, of having something like mathematical accuracy in their structure.

Unlike the real-world theories of magic that they resemble, "hard magic" is inevitably only available to some characters. A real-world magus like John Dee thought that anyone could learn the rules of how the world worked and could use that knowledge so summon angels. In hard magic stories, characters with the right talent follow laid-out rules that enable them to do things. By consuming a certain metal, or touching a certain color, they can achieve a certain effect. Consume a different metal, you get a different effect.

The genealogy of hard magic, in fact, is this:

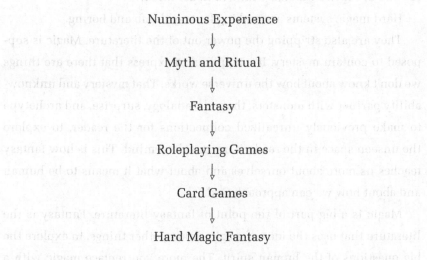

Numinous Experience

↓

Myth and Ritual

↓

Fantasy

↓

Roleplaying Games

↓

Card Games

↓

Hard Magic Fantasy

The game-like rules of hard magic can provide useful constraints for a storyteller constructing a plot. (Ah, sorry, the hero is out of tin, so the villains are going to defeat him. Oh, hey, he saves the day when he realizes that he can use his talent to consume an alloy of tin, like bronze, to get a different effect. Hooray!) But you create two potential problems.

The first problem is that some storytellers think that the whole point of a fantasy novel is to construct a magic system and then devise a scenario in which the hero wins by learning a previously unrealized aspect of the magic system. This is tedious. I wish I were making this up, but I am not. I have spent years talking about fantasy literature at conventions and hand-selling fantasy books at display booths and in bookstores. If I say, "I write fantasy novels," the most common response is, "What's

Real Hard Magic

If you want to read a historical book of magic that is arguably hard magic, and is the grandaddy of Renaissance court grimoires, check out Heinrich Cornelius Agrippa's *Three Books of Occult Philosophy*. It's way more complicated than, "I burn tin."

your magic system?" When young writers come to pitch their stories to me, the most common way they start their pitch is by telling me about their magic systems. When I was on a panel a few years ago at Salt Lake City's FanX and told the audience that I thought hard magic systems were dumb, one guy raised his hands and asked, "If you don't have a hard magic system, how do you have your character come to a new insight at the end of act two that lets him win in act three?"

Hard magic systems are making fantasy dumb and boring.

They are also stripping the power out of the literature. Magic is supposed to contain mystery. It's supposed to express that there are things we don't know about how the universe works. That mystery and unknowability partner with monsters, the gods, analogy, surprise, and archetype to make previously unrealized connections for the reader, to explore the unseen space in the reader's unconscious mind. This is how fantasy teaches us more about ourselves and about what it means to be human and about how we can approach God.

Magic is a big part of the point of fantasy literature. Fantasy is the literature that uses the idea of magic, among other things, to explore the big questions of the human spirit. The more you replace magic with a simplified, dumbed down, superheroish, plastic imitation of magic, the more you turn the books into something that has the form of fantasy, but denies the power thereof.

What's the Alternative?

How do we get away from hard magic? What would a more realistic, more powerful magic look like in a book? What would fantasy look like that got us closer to the myths and legends of the genre's roots? How can we recover the good old stuff and banish the plastic?

Magic is notoriously difficult to define. Etymologically, we get the word from Greek *mageia*, which means the theology of the *magoi*[1], the dream-interpreting Persian priests said to have called on the infant Jesus[2]. This suggests that as we examine the meaning of the word "magic" more deeply, we're going to find connections with religious practice, spirituality, oracles, and things done by outsiders, that is to say, *people other than ourselves.*

A recent study of Jewish magic by Yuval Harari devotes its substantial first chapter to reviewing academic understandings of what magic is from the mid-nineteenth century to date.[3] Harari characterizes the evolving understanding of magic as moving broadly through three trends, or three kinds of theoretical explanations of magic. There is obviously significant overlap among his categories, and I would suggest we should see a fourth category interwoven with the others. What follows is my synthesis and summary of what Harari claims.

Harari describes early theories as evolutionist, meaning that they identify magic as "a stage in the process of spiritual and cultural advancement that humanity undergoes in the course of its development."[4] Some of these theories find the origin of magic in specific human needs (exorcism of spirits, which are the source of all "physical and spiritual problems"[5]) or in posited early beliefs about the structure of reality (in animistic thought, in which all things have individual spirits;[6] or in the allegedly even earlier belief that all things have a collective soul;[7] or in the belief in "the law of participation, which implies a linkage between the individual's personality and things in the world"[8]). Other theorists have tried to identify in magic a pre-modern intellectual phase with some relationship to science and religion, e.g.: that magic is the "original form of human thought," preceding religion, which in turn precedes science;[9] that magic is the "first sign of scientific thought," in that it posits knowable laws of the universe that can be manipulated to achieve results;[10] or conversely that the laws of magic have their origin in religion, where they "serve as part of the perception of holiness and holy powers."[11]

Harari goes on to identify as separate trends sociological and anthropological explanations of magic; for simplicity's sake I'll lump these together. Some theorists have found the definitions of magic in the community of users and non-users, for instance arguing that: religion is how we collectively approach the "lofty and beneficent" gods for help, whereas magic is how we individually approach "inferior and negative entities;"[12] magical acts are externally or physically identical to religious acts, but are socially prohibited;[13] magic is religion before it gets organized, and lone sorcerers are replaced with a priestly caste;[14] or magic is what is performed by people of low or vague social class.[15] Some writers have argued for a calendrical explanation of magic: religion is comprised of acts that are performed cyclically, and magic is undertaken in response to crises.[16] Recent theorists have argued that there is little or no distinction between magic and religion at all: that all magical and religious behavior exists on "a continuum of ritual behavior";[17] that the difference between magic and religion exists only in the eye of the Western observer;[18] or that the difference between magic and religion is purely a semantic problem.[19]

I would extract a fourth category of theories of magic from Harari's summaries, to wit, psychological explanations of magic. Some thinkers have seen magic as "the emotional reaction of primitive man to the anxiety evoked by the surrounding world."[20] Others have seen magic as a psychological tool, protecting the self or "ego" and thereby developing the institution of the individual,[21] ritualizing optimism to confer hope,[22] or imposing order on the world.[23]

Obviously, I have just begun to scratch the surface of what magic is in the real world. No mention is made in the above summary, for example, of the content of real-world grimoires, of magic as initiatic traditons, of what real-world spells actually look like, of the phenomenon of pseudepigraphy, or many other important and interesting issues.

Nevertheless, Harari's summary suggests a criterion by which we may judge the verisimilitude of "magic systems" or otherwise the magic described in a fantasy story. An authentic "magic system" would fit many, or maybe all, of Harari's definitions. In other words, an authentic magic system would be one in which academics who are not themselves practitioners, observing magical practice in the story world, could propose any of the foregoing theories to explain why practitioners do what they do.

To make a few more specific points. An authentic presentation of magic in a novel would look like the following:

1. At some margin, magic should resemble science, with knowable laws and repeatable operations.
2. At some margin, magic should resemble religion. The line separating magical and religious ritual should be difficult to find. One person's magic should be another person's religion.
3. Magic should be connected to social and in-group status (the theology of the stargazers becomes the wizardry of the Greeks).
4. Magic should meet (individual and also collective) psychological needs of those who seek to employ it.

A "hard magic" system certainly could meet our criteria for authenticity. Without conducting any kind of survey, my unscientific impression is that most of them don't, and in fact, don't consciously try. Instead, they are constructed to follow consistent internal logic and provide a system of costs and possibilities for the story setting. What card do I play? How many blue tokens do I need for it to work?

The lack of authenticity in the magic systems of contemporary fantasy is a loss; let's consider again Harari's list. In the real world, magic is intimately connected with the human response to crises (which is to say, growth, heroism, narrative, destruction, change, and initiation). Magic is at some (or all) stages intrinsic to human thought, and it is closely related to human worship. Magic is defined by social lines, and by our perceptions of our own cultures and other cultures.

In other words, magic is tightly connected to the human spirit. Fantasy at its best is the what-if literature of human spirituality, one reason being that magic in the real world is tightly bound to the human soul. Therefore, what-if postulates about authentic magic in a fantasy setting are what-if postulates about our spirit, and the human condition. A "hard magic" system that is rigorous, logical, and consistent, but lacks the ambiguity, sociality, spirituality, visceral psychology, and thought-content of real magic, has taken a long step away from the human soul. To me, candidly, many "hard magic" systems feel like fan fiction for a roleplaying or collectible card game, rather than the mirror to the human condition they should be. Our literature becomes the poorer thereby.[24]

LARPing

LARPing is live action roleplaying. It's the same thing as tabletop roleplaying, conceptually, except that instead of imagining your characters moving around in a visualized imaginary space, or maybe representing those characters with miniatures, or little cardboard chits, you stand and walk about and represent your character physically, as on a stage. If your wizard casts a fireball, you might represent that by throwing a tennis ball at another character.

LARPing is the kind of thing that may get organized on a large scale at old-style fandom science fiction conventions (see p. 38). To "LARP" has also entered the vocabulary of the general population, meaning to fake or pretend to do something.

Grimdark Is the Philosophy of Sophomores

To be honest, I don't know which is worse. Hard magic deprives fantasy of its power of evoking meaning. Grimdark does have meaning, but the meaning is puerile or degrading.

Like hard magic, grimdark fantasy has antecedents. There have long been writers who wanted to tell dark tales in fantasy idioms. A famous example would be the Thieves' World books. This is a sword and sorcery setting created by Robert Asprin and Lynn Abbey to be a shared setting in which many writers could work, each using his own characters or borrowing the characters of other writers with permission and care (see p. 85). Many of the stories are about thieves and cutthroats and thugs, antiheroes who in classic epic fantasy would appear as villains or minor characters or not at all. They are whores and pimps, junkies and dealers, smugglers and fences. (Except, notably, David Drake's character in the first Thieves' World anthology, who comes to town to avenge the mistreatment of his sister by a hermaphrodite posing as a god, and destroys the god and his cult.) Glen Cook's Black Company stories may also be seen as a forerunner to grimdark.

But at a certain point, some fantasy writers began to revel in nihilism. George R.R. Martin is not the only example, but he achieved outsized success, with the TV show *Game of Thrones*, based on his unfinished series *A Song of Ice and Fire*. Martin had a significant background in Hollywood, having worked on *The Twilight Zone* and *Beauty and the Beast* (the TV show with Ron Perlman about the lion-faced man living in the New York City sewers, not the Disney movies).[25] The TV show, spinoffs, action figures, and games have led far too many readers and too many aspiring writers to think that there's something clever or interesting about his series. There isn't. Martin has simply decided that there is no such thing as heroism and he's the man to demonstrate it.

His decision to kill Ned Stark in book one had shock value, but it was the transgressive shock value of pornography. And because the only

The Muse

Here's something they won't tell you in your writing workshops. The Muse is real. When you mock Her by writing garbage, She leaves.

philosophy he had to offer was that heroism is bunk, he had to keep upping the thrills by turning the crank on the wickedness porn. Thus we got the "Red Wedding." Fans who were disappointed in the ending of the TV series, which was mass murder all around, just weren't paying attention. The TV series end is not some aberration from Martin's philosophy, it's the inevitable end of it. Your knights and kings and fantasy heroes are all just murderers, Martin wants to tell you. There are no heroes. You went along with it because it was different and kind of exciting and then there were lots of naked people, but in the end, Martin is a nihilist who hates human beings.

To redeem his series, Martin would have had to show someone rising above, some great redeeming sacrifice that restored order and peace to the universe. But he doesn't believe in that possibility.

Martin has described himself as wanting to argue with Tolkien:

I look at the end and it says Aragorn is the king and he says, 'And Aragorn ruled wisely and well for 100 years' or something. It's easy to write that sentence. But I want to know what was his tax policy, and what did he do when famine struck the land? And what did he do with all those Orcs? A lot of Orcs left over. They weren't all killed, they ran away into the mountains. Sauron fell down, but you see all the Orcs running away. Did Aragorn carry out a policy of systematic Orc genocide? Did he send his knights out into the hills to kill all the Orcs? Even the little baby Orcs? Or was there Orc rehabilitation going on. Trying to teach the Orcs to be good citizens. And if the Orcs were the result of Elves . . . could Orcs and Elves intermarry?[26]

This all adds up to the wisdom of the sophomore, the posturing of the pimpled barely-adult who says he believes in nothing, we're no better than the animals, and hey, wanna sleep with me? The urge to attack

Tolkien is telling—the man-child wants to overthrow and replace the father.

The desire to indict Tolkien also makes the choice between philosophies clear. Tolkien fought in the Great War. His boyhood friends died in the mud in France. He writes about the need for sacrifice and the urgency that the men of the west band together and stand against the mechanized evil of Mordor. Martin, on the other hand, claimed conscience objector status to avoid going to Vietnam and then made a career in Hollywood. He wants us to believe that there are no heroes, that everyone is a potential murderer, out for himself.

I know which world I believe in, and which man I'd rather be.

Chapter Sixteen

THE GREAT PUPPIES CONTROVERSY AND THE CHINESE KNOCKOFF[1]

In 2023, for the second time in ten years, insiders of the World Science Fiction Convention bent their own rules in an attempt to police the bounds of what books and writers are to be seen as acceptable science fiction and fantasy. The second time, they did it on behalf of the Chinese Communist Party.

The Worldcon insiders are a clique of writers and editors associated with a small number of the largest science fiction and fantasy publishers and their friends and allies who work behind the scenes organizing conventions—the SMOFs of fandom. The insiders promptly announced that any idea that the turf-war games they had gleefully engaged in had now gone awry on them was mistaken. For instance, science fiction novelist John Scalzi informed commenters to his blog post on the subject that "Attempts to re-litigate the Sad Puppy nonsense in the comments here will be Malleted." But why would anyone connect the events of Worldcon 81 in Chengdu, China, with the Sad Puppy conflicts?

The previous beating of the bounds took place over a series of Worldcons and is generally known by some reference to the Sad Puppies, who were the principal faction the Worldcon insiders were fighting to excommunicate at the time. The events of the Sad Puppies conflicts became complicated, but at their heart, they're simple, and in their origin, they're personal. Fantasy and science fiction novelist and former gun store owner Larry Correia writes heroic action stories about honorable people fighting monsters (see p. 125). When he first broke into publishing with *Monster Hunter International*, a cheerful story about private companies hunting monsters for government bounties in rural America, he found himself a finalist for the John W. Campbell Award for Best New Writer (to be awarded at Worldcon 69 in Reno, along with the Hugos). Correia expected to go to Worldcon and hang out with like-minded nerdy writers, but even before the event he found himself socially snubbed by a wall of sneering leftism. He was called "an NRA stooge" and a "merchant of death" who liked to "dance in the blood of children." Most famously, he was told that he was "not a real writer," a gibe that Correia's fans to this day repeat with ironic delight.

Worldcon is an annual convention held in a different city every year. At each Worldcon, attendees and also people who pay for non-attending memberships vote where the convention will be held in the future, and also vote to determine who will receive the awards, most famously including the once-prestigious Hugo Awards. Despite this peripatetic nature, Worldcon has a core group of participants who return year after year—"fandom" (see p. 33). Fandom leans left and can be very cliquish. Many fans have been attending Worldcon for decades and see it as something like their science fiction family reunion.

Writers of the Future: Scientology Pitches in

The Church of Scientology has a deep connection with science fiction in the person of its founder, L. Ron Hubbard. Hubbard was a prolific writer across many genres, published in the pulp magazines (see p. 75) and in novel form. Arguably Hubbard's most famous fiction is *Battlefield Earth*, memorably made into a cinematic bomb torturing John Travolta's acting talents as a nine-foot-tall dreadlock-sprouting giant. Er, featuring. I said featuring. I am also delighted that Hubbard composed a soundtrack for the novel, called *Space Jazz*. As of this writing, *Space Jazz* is available on Amazon in mp3 format.

In any case, the Church of Scientology continues to support the artistic field of its founder. Writers and Illustrators of the Future is a quarterly science fiction and fantasy short story and art contest funded the church. The contest's judges are top professionals in their fields, and entry is only open to novices and amateurs. More than one writer's career has been launched by winning Writers of the Future and thereby catching the eye of agents and publishers (though I should say that plenty of winners still remain, so to speak, writers of the future). The contest also has an affiliated podcast that interviews science fiction and fantasy writers about their books and reaches a significant audience.

Correia didn't win the Campbell, but that defeat wasn't enough for the hardcore lefties of fandom, who went after him online (as they continue to do today). In the flame wars that ensued, Correia argued that Worldcon was a small convention and its insiders didn't reflect the thinking of all readers of science fiction and fantasy, so their social snub was unimportant. This is correct, but it violated fandom's image of itself as the community out of which science fiction and fantasy spring. The convention was small enough that it took only a modest number of votes for a book to win one of the convention's coveted Hugo Awards, and even fewer for a book to become a finalist. He confidently predicted that he and his readers could get one of his books in as a finalist for Best Novel, though he expressed doubt that he had enough pull with fandom to make any book a winner. He duly made good on his prediction, and his novel *Warbound* was a finalist for the Hugo Award for Best Novel at Worldcon 72 in London.

At any point, Correia could have walked away. And at any point, the lefty insiders of science fiction could have stopped insulting and threatening him. Neither happened. Instead, with the Worldcon insiders leaning hard into the banner of "diversity" while giving awards to white liberals, Correia put forward a slate of recommendations for Worldcon 73 in Spokane. He called his nominees the "Sad Puppies" slate in a tongue-in-cheek cartoon, warning that "boring message-fic winning awards" was the cause of puppy sadness. Correia maintains that he had no idea what the race or sexual orientation of his nominees were, "we were just picking people who were popular or good but who'd normally get ignored by the leftist cliques." His slate nevertheless included women, ethnic minorities, and people we might today call LGBTQIA+.

Correia's fans and sympathizers voted finalists into multiple categories for the Hugo Awards set to be handed out at Worldcon 73 in Spokane.

This was looming disaster. The Worldcon insiders couldn't bear the thought that any of Correia's slate might win and took action to stuff the ballot box. This was possible because Worldcon allows people who purchase non-attending memberships to vote along with people who attend the convention. Presumably the idea was originally that someone who regularly came to Worldcon but couldn't in a particular year could still support the event by purchasing a (relatively cheap) non-attending membership, and that person should be allowed to vote.

The Hugo voting in 2015 was flooded with non-attending memberships. You can see it in the number of total votes cast: Worldcon 72 (in cosmopolitan London): 3,587, Worldcon 73 (in backwater Spokane): 5,950. Insiders didn't want any of Correia's candidates to win, and insiders bought enough bogus memberships to ensure that it didn't happen. One result was that No Award, a previously little-used ballot option, was the winner in five categories. In five categories, confronted with a list of five eligible finalists, many preferred by hundreds of voters, the ballot-stuffers chose to give the prize to no one.

Finalists for the Hugo for Best Editor, Long Form included Anne Sowards, Toni Weisskopf, and Sheila Gilbert, all powerful and respected women in the field. It also included Vox Day, a right-wing provocateur who was drafting in Correia's wake with his own slate of candidates and further muddying the waters. Toni was Correia's suggested candidate. I'm slightly simplifying the complicated voting process, but Toni won more votes than any previous winner of the Hugo for Best Editor, Long Form, ever had at 1,216 . . . but "No Award" won 2,496. By comparison, Ginjer Buchanan won the award in 2014 with 359 votes. To prevent Vox Day from winning the Hugo, and to show Larry Correia who was boss, the Worldcon insiders threw the award away.

The Lords of Kobol: Why Are There So Many Mormons Here?

It has often been noted that Mormons seem to be overrepresented among writers of SFF literature in recent decades.[2] In no particular order, Orson Scott Card, Zenna Henderson, Stephenie Meyer, Ally Condie, Tracy Hickman, Brandon Sanderson, David Farland Wolverton, Brandon Mull, James Dashner, Larry Correia, Dan Wells, Brad Torgersen, Eric James Stone, and D. J. Butler (!), among others, are all (in at least some sense) Mormon. Mormon creatives have also hit the big screen, most famously in Glen A. Larson's deeply Mormon TV series *Battlestar Galactica* (the remake was notably less Mormon).

Various explanations have been mooted for why this might be the case. Mormons have a rich and distinctive cosmology. Mormons have a tradition of giving broad latitude to individual heterodoxy so long as behavior is orthodox, leading to the existence of many armchair theologians. Mormons strongly value education, resulting in high rates of reading. Mormons have extra books of narrative scripture, so they are even more immersed in narrative-driven meaning than mainstream Christians are. Mormons got in some early successes, who helped or inspired others to follow them. Some or all of these might be at least partially factors.

Also not to be underestimated is the effect of community. The Life, the Universe, and Everything Symposium ("LTUE") held its forty-third annual event in February 2025. LTUE is not specifically Mormon, but it was founded by students of Brigham Young University professor Marion K. "Doc" Smith and for its first thirty years held on BYU campus. It continues to be held every year in Provo, Utah, attracting big-name writers and editors to teach about the craft and business of writing science fiction and fantasy to thousands of attendees. This means that in the geographical heart of Mormondom there is an accessible, cheap, friendly, first-class forum for aspiring SFF writers to learn and network. This also means that Dave Doering, LTUE's principal founder and continuing head, is one of the great SMOFs of all time. It's never boring with Dave Doering!

Fast forward to Worldcon 81, held in 2023 in Chengdu, China. Worldcon sites are chosen by vote two years in advance. In 2021, Worldcon was again flooded with non-participating memberships, and Chengdu, China, was selected as the site for Worldcon 81. It clobbered Winnipeg, 2,006 to 807. Over 1,900 of Chengdu's votes were from non-attending members—i.e., mail-in ballots—and over 1,500 of those didn't even give a street address for the putative voter. The ballot box had been stuffed again, this time to get the convention to China.

Why would China want Worldcon? Danielle Ranucci of the Human Rights Foundation has suggested that the Chinese state was behind the ballot-stuffing and that it wanted to host Worldcon to "launder its reputation, legitimize its genocide, and promote dubious research." Whatever the reason, someone in China wanted Worldcon, and they followed the playbook of the Worldcon insiders themselves to get it.

The in-person event apparently went well, but the scandal doesn't end there: the 2023 Hugo Awards were rigged. Leaked emails and other documents reveal that the Hugo administrators for Worldcon 81 removed from consideration authors and works that they deemed not eligible for a Hugo. Eligibility turns out to have depended on suitability for publication under Chinese censorship laws, Hugo administrator Dave McCarty emailing the rest of the committee to watch out for "mentions of Hong Kong, Taiwan, Tibet, negatives of China." It's not clear whether the administrators were acting at the direction of the Chinese state, or simply taking it on themselves to act as if they were. In an interview after the committee's actions became public, McCarty maintained that he acted within the parameters of the World Science Fiction Society Constitution; if so, it was unprecedented action.

So China didn't choose who won the 2023 Hugos, but Chinese rules determined who wouldn't be allowed to compete.

Worldcon insiders were very upset about all of this. However much they might have disliked him, Correia played fair—the insiders were the ones who bent the rules to win. They managed to defend their playhouse against Correia and his conservative insurgents, only to have China run their own plays back at them, using non-attending memberships and collusion to delegitimize dissenting voices.

Larry Correia's comment on the 2023 Hugos scandal was, "The Chinese communists quietly did the same thing the American lefties did loudly. To the Chinese it wasn't personal, just business as usual. To the Worldcon woke, it was deeply personal, and they gleefully try to ruin the career of any authors who step out of line."

Does any of this really matter in the larger picture? Probably not. Correia's original point stands: Worldcon's fandom is a small community, not to be confused with science fiction readers in general. Whatever agents and editors still attend, Worldcon's fandom doesn't control access to publishing, now less than ever as indie publishing continues to explode and bookstores struggle. A writer could sell tens of thousands of books now and be invisible to fandom. For anyone who is paying attention, the Hugos first went woke and then bowed the knee to authoritarian China. Fandom may wish to act as the gatekeepers of science fiction and fantasy, but they've crippled their credibility.

Master Li and Number Ten Ox

China has made a splash in speculative fiction before. A delightful book that would be difficult to publish in the current age of obsession over own stories and cultural appropriation is Barry Hughart's *Bridge of Birds*, a tale of an ancient and fantastic China in which the main characters are sages, monks, and burly farmers.

Chapter Seventeen

SFF CONQUERS THE WORLD; FANDOM HURT MOST

Some of the background of the Hugos controversy is an argument over what fandom means. A large background factor in the discussion was a titanic sea-change in who is consuming science fiction and fantasy.

Historically, fantasy and especially science fiction have been principally intramural literatures, written and read by the same people. (This is obviously a generalization, but it is nevertheless broadly true.) There have always been books that broke out of those constraining walls. Tolkien was never captured within them. *Dhalgren* probably sold as well as it did because it got beyond fandom. Harry Potter, a work for children but a work that aged upward into young adult territory and a work that was undeniably about wizards, reached the entire world.

Those successes came along with other successes in the popular culture. Tabletop roleplaying games escaped from the dungeon and became the hobby of rock musicians and movie stars (see sidebar on p. 130).

Movies and TV shows got made. Some of them looked great and truly were great (*Star Wars*, *Battlestar Galactica*). Some of them looked ridiculous but found a niche audience and hung on (*Doctor Who*, *Star Trek*). Some of them were just awful (*Starcrash*, *Battle Beyond the Stars*). There was a fantasy film craze in the 1980s, producing a few genuine classics (*Ladyhawke*, *The Last Unicorn*, *Highlander*) and a lot of movies that, at best, are entertaining trash (*Hawk the Slayer*).

Over time, the walls have broken down. Science fiction and fantasy no longer live in their own little garden, the property of a discrete club of people who want others to like what they like but also want to retain control over it. This was at the heart of the dispute between Larry Correia and the Hugo insiders (see p. 141). Larry's basic argument was that he knew he wasn't an insider, but he didn't care, because he could sell a lot of books anyway.

Media Tie-ins, Store-bought and Homemade

Some people just can't escape their favorite movies (or, to be fair, literature). Sometimes this state of being trapped leads a fan to write her own Star Wars / Star Trek / Harry Potter / Lord of the Rings stories, which may be posted online or shared in a fanzine. Such "fan fic" may simply allow a reader to write continuing adventures, but it also may permit the exploration of alternative endings or romantic relationships that never occurred to the original author.

Publishers are happy to capitalize on this desire to stay engaged with a successful media property and regularly publish authorized "tie-in" novels of large media properties, such as Alien, Star Wars, Star Trek, etc. A great deal of work goes into maintaining consistency across multiple novels by multiple authors, policing what is "canon" in a fictional universe. Fantastically, one of the world's biggest media franchises has twice thrown away and rebooted its entire tie-in universe. That franchise is Star Wars.

The first time Star Wars rebooted itself may have escaped your notice, because it happened a long time ago, and in a galaxy far, far away. I kid. It happened in 1980, with the release of *The Empire Strikes Back*. Because, you see, *Star Wars Episode IV: A New Hope* (or, as we old people call it, "*Star Wars*") already had a sequel. That sequel was a book called *Splinter in the Mind's Eye*, and it was written by Alan Dean Foster. Foster had written the novelization of *Star Wars* and was also hired to write in novel form a sequel that would be cheap and easy to film, in case *Star Wars* did well enough to merit a film sequel, but not well enough to get a big budget. He also couldn't use Han Solo, because Harrison Ford hadn't signed up to any more films at that point.

He could, however, use and ramp up the sexual tension between Luke and Leia, which he did, because, of course, none of us knew yet that they were brother and sister. Apparently Lucas didn't know either, because he didn't ask Foster to change any of those passages. He also didn't ask Foster to change the duel scene in which Luke sliced off Darth Vader's arm. Instead, when *Star Wars* was a mega hit and *Empire* got a lot of funding, Lucas obliterated *Splinter in the Mind's Eye* entirely by publishing it but also ignoring it, effectively decanonizing *Star Wars*' first tie-in novel at launch. Star Wars rebooted itself for its second film.

Star Wars rebooted itself again for *Star Wars Episode VII: The Great Cash Grab*. In the intervening years, many Star Wars tie-in novels had been written, notably including Dave Wolverton's *The Courtship of Princess Leia*, Timothy Zahn's beloved books about the post-*Return of the Jedi* Imperial threat, Admiral Thrawn, and the Young Jedi Knights books by Kevin J. Anderson and Rebecca Moesta. The setting and timeline as narrated in these many novels was collectively known as the "Expanded Universe." J. J. Abrams, Kathleen Kennedy, and team happily ignored and therefore bulldozed the entire Expanded Universe with the most expensive fan fic ever, *Star Wars Episode VII: The Same Old Hope*. Episode VII treated us to the spectacle of Abrams having the fun of remaking *Star Wars* as he would have made it, complete with Death Star. Except that he had to kill Han Solo, because by this time Harrison Ford just wasn't having more of it. And who was going to stop them? The young Jedi are all dead and therefore can't complain; Leia has also been safely killed off and has no further need of a courtship. Admiral Thrawn, at least, was popular enough that Zahn was brought back to reboot him in the new Star Wars Universe 3.0.

Faithful Epics

SFF books have become mainstream and have gotten faithful film adaptations. This is an ouroboric chicken and egg relationship and I won't attempt to discern which trend is cause and which effect. In recent years,

Jonathan Strange and Mr Norell and *Gormenghast* have both been made into fantastic TV miniseries by the BBC.

One obvious bigger example is *The Lord of the Rings*. It was first filmed in 1978 by Ralph Bakshi, who made an animated feature that had insufficient support from the film studios to complete the series, so it ended at the Battle of Helm's Deep (if you have not yet read *The Lord of the Rings*, that means that he only filmed the first two books of the trilogy). Fun fact: Mick Jagger wanted to play Frodo, but he threw his hat into the ring too late.[1] Famously, the film pioneered rotoscoping technology, which filmed actors live and then painted over the filmed images to make the animation.

Video Mutates the Novel Star

The success in recent years of streaming as a medium of long-form storytelling may affect the shape of future novels. Past writing students learned a three-act Hollywood structure with which to build their plots, but now writers have to consider how their story looks in five to seven acts, to conform to the outline of a streamed series.

When the animated film was completed in 1980 with *The Return of the King*, it was by different animators, using different animation technology, and in an entirely different style. Fans loved the two films, but mostly because that was all they were likely to get, not because the films were in themselves amazing.

Peter Jackson's *The Lord of the Rings* trilogy, by contrast, is amazing. It is broadly faithful to Jackson's themes and vision while also successful converting Tolkien's poetic language and descriptions into action films that hold the audience's attention despite being long. One can pick nits. The attempt to make Arwen Undomiel's part bigger by having her bring the reforged sword to Aragon was well-intentioned but it had knock-on effects that undermined Tolkien's themes—in the book, the oathbreakers answer Aragon's call to come save Minas Tirith because they owe their oath to him as king, but in the movie they do it because he carries a magic sword. This is a dumbing-down and a miss, but it's a tiny misstep in what is generally a colossal success that was seen by pretty much the entire planet.

Dune has been filmed not twice, but three times (and almost four). The first was David Lynch's surreal, internalized, mystical film in 1984, with its many voiceovers, its aesthetic of the grotesque, and its odd interpretation of the Weirding Way as a sonic weapon rather than as a martial art. Second came the Sci Fi Channel's first miniseries, an adaptation that was linear, faithful, and low-budget-looking. Finally, in two parts, we've had Denis Villeneuve's version, which, like Jackson's fantasy epic, manages to be both beautiful on the screen and *generally* faithful to the source material . . . at least until the end.

The film vision of *Dune* that never happened was a psychedelic monsterpiece proposed but never made by Alejandro Jodorowsky. It was supposed to star, fun fact, Mick Jagger, along with David Carradine, Orson Wells, and others. Concept art by H. R. Giger went on to be influential in the *Alien* franchise. Though this *Dune* was never realized, it did result in a spectacular documentary, *Jodorowsky's Dune*, about the attempt.

Apparently, they are also now going to remake Harry Potter, as a streamed series this time. Given the way Hollywood had already rushed to remake *A Series of Unfortunate Events* and *The Golden Compass*, I shouldn't be surprised. I would have thought that Rowling already had her faithful, good-looking, big-screen adaptation, but I supposed one can never be too cynical about Hollywood.

Maybe they'll go the other direction and remake the stories as low-budget animation.

Videogames as Literature

As the processing, graphics, and sound capabilities and memory of gaming platforms have increased, videogames have become a vehicle for long-form storytelling. There are career SFF writers making a living working principally or even exclusively for gaming companies. There are also big-name novelists who have made significant contributions to the storylines and characters of videogames, including: Harlan Ellison, Orson Scott Card, Douglas Adams, George R.R. Martin, Terry

Pratchett, and Neil Gaiman. I worry about the effect of this on the literature, to be candid. In the same way that I think that the success of games like Dungeons & Dragons and Magic: The Gathering led to the debased oddity of so-called "hard magic," I think that a generation (of men, to generalize) whose principal consumption of storytelling has been in the form of videogames has led to readers who get very excited if the end of every chapter includes a character sheet for the protagonist and an explanation of how he's spending the experience earned in the chapter.

Too Much of a Good Thing

Superheroes on the big screen are nothing new. *Superman and the Mole Men* came out in 1951, and in 1978 Christopher Reeves as the big fella was a smash hit. Batman fought foreign saboteurs as early as the 1940s and has been rebooted multiple times since, most recently played by an actor more famous for incarnating a hunky vampire.

But there's never been anything quite like the Marvel Cinematic Universe, or MCU. The movies were great at first. I liked *Iron Man* and the early Avengers movies. *Guardians of the Galaxy* made it look like they wouldn't take themselves too seriously and could avoid getting trapped in their own pattern. And then, under the commercially savvy leadership of the Walt Disney Corporation, the joyous four-color underground art of creators like Stan Lee and Jack Kirby has been ground up, injected with Joss Whedon snark, and spewed out as a multiverse of pink slime on the world. The project is currently in phase six, comprising in all dozens of films and TV shows as well as toys, games, costumes, and every other conceivable kind of merchandise.

On the one hand, part of me is grateful. Marvel has dug so deep into its material that even lesser characters like my favorites, Power Man and Iron First, have had their own shows. Not just shows, but action figures and LEGO sets. On the other hand, the shows have degraded over time, becoming formulaic, hackneyed, and woke (*She-Hulk: Attorney at Law*, I'm looking at you). And they don't seem to be stopping.

The tight-wearing heroes of the MCU have become the dominating gods of modern mass media culture. There are other gods, but the MCU's pantheon rules. The media conventions, Comic Cons and their ilk, are their annual festivals. Worshippers come to the holy sites to see the great priestesses and priests, to wear the clothing of the gods, to make offerings, and to circumambulate in joyous reverence with the faithful.

It's all a bit too much.

Maybe we should be grateful that DC's attempts to launch its competitor 'verse have been a failure by contrast.

Lie Down with Dogs

The problem with Hollywood success is that it brings Hollywood problems. In the late 2010s and early 2020s, one of the great Hollywood problems has been wokeness. Some big notable Hollywood fantasy projects have been tainted by it.

I should confess that I have never read *The Wheel of Time*. When fans describe it, it just doesn't sound good to me. So I set out to watch the recent show, thinking it would spark my enthusiasm and I'd finally read the books. But the show started in a little remote mountain village, where, like a human shelf of Heinz beans, there were fifty-seven varieties of human ethnicity, all shades and colors.

Because that's how little remote mountain villages work. They attract a cosmopolitan array of ethnic groups.

I sighed and kept watching. Then I hit the part where women can do magic and be fine, but if men do magic, they go insane. Fine, that's a nice dramatic setup, you can do interesting things with it. Oh, and also, we're waiting for a prophesied figure called the Dragon Reborn to return, and the Dragon Reborn will defeat the baddies, and the Dragon Reborn can be either a man or a woman.

I stopped and phoned a friend who knew the Wheel of Time. "They

Wearing the Cape

Traditional publishing has had a hard time selling superhero novels, including tie-ins, so writers of those books have found themselves in the indie space. Check out *Wearing the Cape* by Marion G. Harmon and *Indomitable* by J. B. Garner.

changed it, didn't they?" I asked. "The story only makes sense if the Dragon Reborn has to be a man. That way we're waiting for a Messiah, but when he comes, he'll be insane. But the filmmakers couldn't stand the idea that the Dragon Reborn couldn't be a woman, so they changed it. And thereby they made the idea stupid and pointless."

My friend confirmed that the filmmakers had indeed changed this point from the underlying book, and I stopped watching.

You knew *The Lord of the Rings: The Rings of Power* was going to be a hot woke mess that didn't care about Tolkien's world at all from the way the studio sold it. Ditzy influencers announced their love for their girl Galadriel and said it was good the show was bringing diversity to Tolkien's work. Unfortunately, what it actually brought was stupidity, girl boss logic, and disregard for Tolkien's canon. If you like this show, God bless you. It isn't Tolkien. It isn't the Silmarillion or the appendices to the Lord of the Rings, it's the filmmakers' own "amazing, untold" story about a character named Galadriel who can climb icy waterfalls but not lead, swim oceans but not recognize the enemy Sauron when he appears. This is not Tolkien's Galadriel, it's a *She-Hulk* secondary character wearing her skin. Hey Amazon, Gandalf's name comes from the Völuspá; it isn't fan service to pretend that the Hobbits named him by calling him Grand Elf, it's just a weird conceit that dismisses the seriousness of Tolkien and infantilizes the Hobbits at the same time.

There's definitely a silver lining here. Fantasy films only have these problems because the genre has gone mainstream. It's only worth the time of filmmaking ideologues to try to turn Tolkien's pre-history into woke pap because Tolkien's is a global household name. And if we can endure and ignore enough bad fantasy films, maybe we'll get good ones again.

Chapter Eighteen

THE CRAZY YEARS

I n Robert Heinlein's fictional (then-future) universe, the end of the twentieth and the beginning of the twenty-first century are known as the "Crazy Years." He described rapid social change leading to insanity. It's a commonplace response to oddity in fandom to shrug one's shoulders and say, "We are living in Heinlein's Crazy Years."

Gold Rush in Publishing

Fortunes were (allegedly) made in the 1849 gold rush by people selling pans and picks and blue jeans to the miners, most of whom impoverished themselves. Similarly, in today's publishing gold rush set off by the revolution in self-publishing technology, many people make their fortunes selling to the writers rather than selling writing. Some of these services simply represent the disaggregation of the bundle of services that publishers would provide, so that a self-publishing author can purchase à la carte the service she thinks she needs to publish her book—editing, cover art and design, layout, marketing.

Other services seem to me to be more predatory, aimed to take advantage of a new writer's lack of knowledge. Career consulting, for instance, is notably offered mostly by people who do not have successful writing careers. Sensitivity reading is bunk. Still others are illicit (e.g., paying for reviews) or scams (e.g., paying an "agent" to read your manuscript). My best advice to new writers is to band together in a writing group with peers. Share all information among you and go to bat for each other. If you have to wonder whether or not you should be paying for something, you probably shouldn't.

The Age of Unfinished Epics: Rothfuss and Martin, et al.

Fantasy, including epic fantasy, once came in trilogies. It never came *exclusively* in trilogies, but, possibly modeling themselves on Tolkien's *The Lord of the Rings*, fantasy writers in the seventies and eighties put out books in sets of three. The Chronicles of Thomas Covenant, the original Shannara Trilogy, Mercedes Lackey's Arrows Trilogy, and many more, were conceived and published as discrete arcs told over three books. (Ironically, *The Lord of the Rings* itself was written as a single book and broken into six volumes; it was published as a trilogy at the insistence of the publisher.)

In the twentieth century, though, epic fantasies became a thing that was done in long series, and in particular, in series that did not finish. Robert Jordan died before finishing *The Wheel of Time*, but his widow selected Brandon Sanderson (who published an appreciation of Jordan's work upon his death) to finish the series.[1] Perhaps attempting to imitate Jordan, writers such as Patrick Rothfuss, Saladin Ahmed, Scott Lynch, George Martin, and even Orson Scott Card have let series languish for years without finishing them. In some cases, the writers have turned to other projects. In some cases, they've stopped writing. In Martin's case, he went back to TV, even finishing his flagship series as a TV-only ending, with no hint that he's likely ever to write the last books.

Life is complicated, art is hard, and there are lots of reasons why a writer might not produce an expected book. This chronic failure of high-profile fantasy series to finish has damaged reader trust, though. I have personally been told by hundreds of browsing readers that they'll pick up a new series "when it's finished." That's their privilege, of course. And the failure of those writers is an opportunity for someone else to pick up the readers. Larry Correia's final volume of his epic fantasy series, Saga of the Forgotten Warrior, carried the following dedication:

"To George R. R. Martin. See? It's not that hard."

The Identity Obsession

I'm not going to name names here.

But it's been a sad carnival of awful, watching the traditional publishers announce that they would choose writers on the basis of ethnic background, sexual preference, or gender identity. It's been depressing to see them carry through with that program, and agents necessarily fall into line, every agent changing her "looking for" list to a grab-bag of politically-favored identities. It's been painful to see successful and beloved midlist writers kicked to the curb by their publishers because they didn't fit the explicitly political mold of people the publishers wished to be publishing. It's been hard, but clarifying, to see the major prizes given out on the basis of identitarian politics. It's been infuriating to watch the bestselling writers who don't fit the identitarian mold but are protected by their sales numbers pretend this hasn't been happening.

The truth is that publishing responds to financial incentives eventually, but only eventually. Publishers and editors are more sensitive to incentives like peer approval, accolades, and prizes. That's why they went into publishing. So I don't think this woke tide in publishing is over yet, to be honest, but the tide may be turning.

Malazan

A well-regarded epic fantasy series of recent years that may be grimdark but has the virtue of being finished is Steven Erikson's Malazan Book of the Fallen, the first volume of which is *Gardens of the Moon*.

The New Ham and Eggs Circuit: Podcasts, Booktubers, Patreon, Discord, etc.

Let me share a personal narrative. I was standing in a hotel suite in Atlanta on Labor Day weekend, 2017, during Dragon Con. The suite had been rented by writer and scientist Robert E. Hampson and was full of people (by which I mean nerds) enjoying light refreshment and conversation.

Science fiction legend Jerry Pournelle (whom I had never met, but whose books I knew) was sitting on a sofa across the room, talking to someone else, and I was standing with Baen Books editor Jim Minz. Abruptly, Pournelle stood up and walked over to me. He looked up at me (I'm taller than he was; I'm taller than most people), said, "Oh, you're not who I thought I was," and then proceeded to talk to me for over two hours.

I share this story to say that this is some of the delight of fandom. Utterly without effort on my part, I had a serendipitous, personal, lengthy encounter with a living legend of science fiction. Just a week later, Pournelle passed away, and but for that chance encounter, I'd never have met him at all.

Also, I want to share something Pournelle told me in that conversation. He demurred at the suggestion that he was a great writer, and insisted that all his success had come from hard work—not in the production of books, which he certainly did, but in marketing. He was a physicist, and he told me that every time NASA did anything, he'd call around to every radio show he could and volunteer to go on the show to explain what NASA was up to. The shows would then incidentally mention his novels, which would drive sales. Pournelle called this "doing the ham and eggs circuit," which I take to mean something like, "persisting in doing the hard work of promoting over time."

There still is a ham and eggs circuit for writers. It includes actual radio shows, and also podcasts (writers, you might take a tip from Jerry Pournelle and seek to be expert in something that will get you on podcasts to discuss something *other* than your fiction), and YouTube channels. The ham and eggs circuit also includes a writer's own Patreon or Discord server or Facebook fan groups where the writer can interact with readers. Doing the work of repeatedly putting yourself out on the ham and eggs circuit is not going to make something you write take off virally and get a movie deal.

Instead, it will slowly but surely add to the number of people reading your books and reading about you and your books. Working the ham and eggs circuit is an investment of time in the long-term outcome.

An example of a writer who has invested well in the ham and eggs circuit, becoming a favorite among booktubers (YouTube channels specializing in reviewing books) and gaining a dedicated and interactive fan base is Christopher Ruocchio (see p. 60).

The Return of Hard Science Fiction

A more cheerful trend in the Crazy Years is that hard science fiction has flouted publisher expectations and continued to sell. Kim Stanley Robinson is characterized as a left-wing and utopian writer of hard science fiction. His themes include economic visions that are alternatives to large corporation-dominated capitalism and the interplay between ecology and culture. These themes play out in nearish future tales in which the settlement of space is sometimes told using the mythology of the settlement of the American West.[2]

Robinson's Mars trilogy covers approximately eighty years (starting in 2026, so here we come!) and speculates about the terraforming of Mars. Characters in the novel debate the priorities and ethics of terraforming, but the action in the story ultimately revolves around the machinations of transnational corporations that control Earth to control the red planet as well. That makes the trilogy a kind of sequel or intellectual response to Heinlein's *The Moon Is a Harsh Mistress*, but where Heinlein saw the moon freeing itself to live in a kind of rugged libertarian society, Robinson envisions the massive corporations crushed by nature itself and a healthy Mars as populated by something more like small autonomous collectives.

Andy Weir's story is the convergence of two lines. One line is the resurgence of hard science fiction. His debut novel *The Martian* was rejected because literary agents didn't think there was demand for a story about an astronaut stranded on Mars and trying to live long enough for a rescue mission to pick him up. The other line is the rise of indie publishing, including self-publishing. As mentioned above (see p. xiv), Weir famously crowdsourced his science, asking for advice online so as to make his science as plausible as it could possibly be (in good scientific fashion, some of his proposals for how things would have worked for Mark Watney have already been falsified). When he failed to get an agent, he published the book as a serial on his blog, then as a kindle e-book. The e-book took off on Amazon, then he sold the audio rights, then finally he sold the print rights. Everything about this story is backward, from a traditional point of view. Weir gave away the story first, which allowed him to sell it in digital form, then audio, and the physical book was last.

Except for the movie, of course. That was even more last.

Another hard science fiction story that has come to the screen recently is *The Expanse*. The unconventionality in the development of *The Expanse* is that it began as a game setting developed by one of the two authors who write together as James S. A. Corey. Like Heinlein and Robinson, Corey sees war breaking out within our more fully-settled solar system. Corey then pushes the story beyond the solar system by envisioning a hub of wormholes, built by a lost alien civilization, like a Grand Central Terminal allowing connections all over the galaxy. Thus *The Expanse* leads into stories of settling the stars.

Dennis E. Taylor's indie hard science fiction Bobiverse starts with the self-published novel *We Are Legion (We Are Bob)*. Bob dies shortly after having his consciousness recorded in a cutting-edge process aimed at allowing eventual revivification of the body. Bob is not revivified in a new, healed body. Instead, his mind is uploaded into computer hardware, and he is launched into space as part of a race to find habitable worlds for humanity. On the way he develops his own ambitions and finds competitors and threats from Earth. He finds his best allies in making copies of himself. Lots and lots of copies. This is a hard science fiction about artificial intelligence, the human soul, and the fine line between.

Indie Publishing and the Proliferation of Microgenres

Indie publishing has been a factor in the revival of hard science fiction. It has also become the primary home for genres not favored by traditional publishing in its current mood, such as military science fiction and military fantasy. There are communities of readers now that thrive outside of fandom and also outside of traditional publishing, reading books in extensive series published by presses like Galaxy's Edge Press and Chris Kennedy Publishing.

So one way that fandom lost its tight grip on science fiction and fantasy literature was that the books burst out of fandom to reach mainstream readers and movie watchers. Another way that fandom lost control was that the means of publishing became cheap and accessible, and new publishers sprang up to serve readers who didn't feel served by the status quo.

A striking way that happens now is that Amazon serves as a tool for surfacing subgenres for which there is more demand than supply. Here's how it works. Indie publishers (self-publishing writers or small press owners) spend lots of time examining and thinking about the Amazon rankings. From time to time, they find a book that seems sui generis, unique, its own kind of thing. Call such a book a unicorn. A unicorn is typically self-published, though it doesn't have to be. One interesting sign of a unicorn is that a book is objectively bad by ordinary criteria but sells lots of copies anyway—that suggests that readers are seeing something in it that they want, that is not quality.

The hypothesis is that readers exist who really liked the unicorn, and they would want more books like the unicorn. The unicorn wranglers then analyze the unicorn to determine its "tropes," i.e., the conventions

Interplanetary Civil War

If you liked *The Expanse*, check out *Metaplanetary* (and its sequel, *Superluminal*), by Tony Daniel. It's exciting hard science fiction about intra-solar system civil war.

Carl

As of this writing, the undisputed king of these Amazon-born neo-genres is Dungeon Crawler Carl, which regularly tops the Bookscan lists.

that define it, and they begin producing literature in volume with the same tropes. If the unicorn is in fact not a fluke, a new genre is born, and for the first people into the genre, it's usually a goldmine. This is how writers discovered and began producing LitRPG, Harem, Reverse Harem, Progression Fantasy, Dungeoncore, and other genres.

To be candid, talking with the people who produce these books is sometimes infuriating. Focusing on "hitting the tropes" exactly right often means producing literature that is by ordinary standards, by *my* standards, *bad*.

But it doesn't have to be bad.

Punk Rock Movements

Another thing that happens in the indie publishing space is that people create magazines, publishers, and series focusing on ideas they feel have been ideologically excluded from traditional publishing. One example is #PulpRev, the Pulp Revolution. The idea driving #PulpRev is that science fiction went wrong after John W. Campbell and the pulps. #PulpRev wants to make science fiction and fantasy fun again, by looking back to the golden age of the pulps. James Alderdice is a #PulpRev writer whose nine-book Brutal Sword Saga is an attempt to return fantasy literature to its muscular pulp roots, often with overtones of the Spaghetti Westerns or Toshiro Mifune films. The first book in the series, *Brutal*, begins when a nameless mercenary others call the "Sellsword" rides into a town on the brink of open war between two wizards. The Sellsword wants nothing to do with either, until the duchess catches his eye . . . and he realizes that she's going to need protection.

#IronAge is a hashtag frequently found advertising the same books and writers as #PulpRev. #IronAge sometimes seems to have a death-metal, Scandinavian aesthetic attached to it, but I've also seen #IronAge Westerns and other genres. The core ethic seems to be the rejection of the dumbing-down of corporate-owned IPs, and the aesthetic's most prominent champion is a YouTuber whose nom de cyber, Razor Fist, is also his pen name. His two-volume series of revolution and intrigue starts with the fantasy noir story *The Long Moonlight*.

Superversive (I generally don't see this as a hashtag) is a literary movement in indie publishing to deliberately fight nihilism in SFF literature by writing stories deliberately promoting noble and traditional virtues. Richard Paolinelli is an example of a superversive science fiction writer and publisher. His novel *Escaping Infinity* is about a hotel that turns out to be an interdimensional portal that summons guests to fight as the champions of all humanity.

Obviously, these three might all overlap. There are others. You'll also see new genres employed by these movements, such as Noblebright (which the antithesis of Grimdark, believing in heroism and hope in a fantasy story) or Solarpunk (the rebuttal to Cyberpunk, believing in a hopeful future, albeit generally in a collectivist one).

Chapter Nineteen

NOW WHAT?

I f you've reached this point in the book with the impression that science fiction and fantasy literature are an ongoing dialog among people who more or less sometimes know each other, who often disagree, and who sometimes disagree violently over big ideas, then I have accurately conveyed to you how I see it.

Now that you know that this conversation exists, what should or can you do about it? Let me wind up with some specific invitations.

Read Working Writers

To some extent, this book is about dead or . . . let's call them "veteran" . . . writers. I certainly encourage you to read Tolkien and Wolfe, especially if you have not read them before. I also want to invite you to read writers who are still working. A writer who sells a book while he's alive can write more books to spread his point of view. And also, feed his children.

You should read *The Sun Eater*, by Christopher Ruocchio. The first book (of seven) is *Empire of Silence*. By the time these words are published, all seven books should be out or almost out. Ruocchio writes grand space opera or space fantasy. The technology is hard (-ish), travel between worlds taking many years, for instance, so that the patrician classes of the Empire are genetically or medically modified for extraordinary lifespans. But there are also extraordinary things in this story that effectively amount to magic—the protagonist eventually develops what we might call superhuman powers, with no real explanation why.

Because an explanation why would be beside the point. Hadrian Marlowe is the scion of a minor noble house who is essentially exiled from his home and gets caught up in first one, and then two simultaneous wars for the existence of mankind. On the one hand, Marlowe announces from the outset that he is the one who murdered the entire race of the Cielcin, the first spacefaring sentients mankind ever met (this declaration makes it jarring when we meet Marlowe and discover his exuberant youthful enthusiasm for Cielcin lore). As mercenary, as agent for the Empire, and as outlaw, Marlowe prosecutes the war against the anthropophagous hermaphrodites who seek no quarter and give none, but come ravening without warning out of space in enormous ships hollowed out of whole asteroids. And on the other hand, Marlowe comes to learn that this is not the real war. The Cielcin are agents of a dead empire whose ruins have been found everywhere in the galaxy, and who fought, and are still fighting, a battle against a mysterious power that fights from its reinforced position at the end of time.

If success has many fathers, the literary fathers of Christopher Ruocchio include Tolkien, Herbert, Wolfe, Peake, and others. These men didn't agree with each other, and Ruocchio in turn doesn't agree with all of them. But he's joined the dialog with a voice that is engaging, provocative, Christian, and maybe above all, grand.

Martin L. Shoemaker writes hard science fiction. His Near-Earth Mysteries (two books so far) are detective stories set on a spaceship (book one) and Mars (book two). His novel *Today I am Carey* is a hard SF exploration of what caretaking for dementia patients looks like in a world in which humanoid robots powered by artificial intelligence can detect changes in the perceptions of the patient and respond by simulating the people the patients believe they are with. Martin is thoughtful, technically sophisticated, and a really strong writer.

I'm going to recommend a third writer, and this recommendation comes with a bittersweet note. I'd only met Howard Andrew Jones in the summer of 2023, as Baen Books (where I was Consulting Editor) was publishing his *Lord of a Shattered Land*. This is the first book of a planned five of the Chronicles of Hanuvar. Howard's protagonist Hanuvar is one part Conan the Barbarian and one part Hannibal of Carthage, an aged general who was once a mighty warrior and still retains his keen mind, which he needs as he sets about recovering his defeated and enslaved people. I listened to Howard read from *Lord of a Shattered Land*, and his reading moved both him and me to tears. He was utterly unironic in the emotion of his narrative as he read this fictional character's words, his own words, about missing his now-destroyed homeland. I bought the book immediately.

In the summer of 2024, I had the chance to sit with Howard and talk for an hour. We became friends easily, finding we had a lot in common in terms of our parallel careers, struggling to find audiences for fiction we cared about. He had finished books two and three of the Chronicles of Hanuvar and was excited to get to the rest of the series.

Just weeks later, I learned that he'd been diagnosed with fast-acting, terminal brain cancer, and that he wasn't expected to leave the hospital.

So there will be no books four and five of the Chronicles of Hanuvar, or if there are, someone else will have written them. Hanuvar's people remain scattered and unredeemed, and Howard Andrew Jones, a brilliant writer of sword and sorcery who has not yet reached the audience he deserves, has been taken from us early. I celebrate the books that Howard has given us.

Life is tragic, and life is also good.

What Is a "'Verse"?

One of the recurring patterns in this book is that a writer will write multiple series in a single fictional universe (see, e.g., Poul Anderson on p. 74, Larry Niven on p. 71). Some writers in fact connect more or even all of their works in a single setting (e.g., Terry Brooks and Brandon Sanderson). Such a fictional universe usually gets a name and can be referred to colloquially as a "'verse." Not all writers have 'verses (Tim Powers does not, unless the real world is a 'verse).

Be an Engaged Reader

The basic thing is to read the books. That's the most important invitation in this chapter.

But we can all do more, even as readers. Book-storytelling risks being replaced by memes, tiktoks, X-halations (?), streaming series, Instagram posts, and many other forms of attention-grabbing media. I invite you to promote books. Give them as gifts. Recommend books you like to book clubs and to teachers. Casually recommend them to other people for no reason at all. Post reviews online. Follow authors in social media and reshare what they say to help them extend their reach. Reach out to the authors and tell them that you care about what they wrote.

Be a Writer

New publishing technology means that nothing ever goes out of print. Every day, the set of books and writers you compete against gets bigger than the day before. Competition has never been fiercer, and that's hard.

On the other hand, it's never been easier to get published. Yes, publishing is something of a clique, and traditional SFF publishing is a clique too, but it's possible to enter those cliques, even without living in

New York. And it's possible—in fact, it's easy—to publish on your own, belonging to no clique at all, or starting your own clique.

If you have a vision you want to share, you live in an age in which no one can stop you from sharing it. That's amazing. Do it.

Get Involved

One reason I have described the sociality of SFF literature and fandom in this book (principally in the sidebars) is to help you see how to make contact with it. If you want to share the SFF literature of the future, that's easy, too. Go to conventions and volunteer. Get on panels as a fan or as an expert in anything relevant that you do. Volunteer to work behind the scenes; you may find that you start out running errands, but if you persist, you'll get more and more responsibility, until you're picking the programming, choosing the award winners, organizing the conventions.

In all things, the future belongs to those who show up. That's true in politics, and it's true in speculative fiction.

ABOUT THE AUTHOR AND HIS BOOKS

I'm an editor. I've worked as the Acquisitions Editor for WordFire Press and a Consulting Editor for Baen Books, and am now Senior Editor of ARK Press, a new genre publisher launching in 2025.

I also write science fiction and fantasy. With no attempt to be exhaustive, if you're interested in speculative fiction, here are some things of mine you might try.

As D. J. Butler, I write SFF for grownups.

The Witchy War is an epic fantasy series set in a magical Jacksonian America. Young Sarah Calhoun discovers that she is the hidden heir of the murdered empress, Mad Hannah Penn, and now her uncle the Emperor wants her dead. Even worse, the violent and deranged god of the Mississippi River, the Heron King Simon Sword, wants to marry her. Book one is *Witchy Eye*.

The Cunning Man and sequels (co-written with Aaron Michael Ritchey) tell the story of Hiram Woolley, a Utah sugar beet farmer who uses his Grandma Hettie's traditional magical lore to battle the demons of the Great Depression.

In the Palace of Shadow and Joy and sequels are sword and sorcery tales about Indrajit and Fix, two thinking men trying not to descend to the level of thugs. Indrajit is the last epic poet of a dying people looking without luck for a successor. Fix left his monastery for love that was not returned. Now they try hard to be heroes in a corrupt old city in which all the incentives are for them to be villains.

As Dave Butler, I write for young readers.

The Kidnap Plot is book one of the trilogy The Extraordinary Journeys of Clockwork Charlie. This is Pinocchio reimagined as a steampunk adventure tale. Charlie's father is kidnapped by trolls. When Charlie goes to rescue him, he learns that the kidnappers are also plotting against Queen Victoria, and that Charlie himself is not a flesh and blood boy at all, but a boy made of springs and gears.

Find me on X at @davidjohnbutler.

ENDNOTES

Introduction

1 John Clute and John Grant eds. *The Encyclopedia of Fantasy*. New York: St. Martin's Press, 1997. John Clute and Peter Nicholls eds. *The Encyclopedia of Science Fiction*. London: Orbit, 1993.

2 McGilchrist, Ian. *The Master and His Emissary: The Divided Brain and the Making of the Western World*. New Haven: Yale University Press, 2009, 32–93.

3 Umberto Eco. *Il nome della rosa*. Milano: Bompiani, 2006, 507.

4 Taleb, Nassim. *Antifragile: Things that Gain from Disorder*. New York: Random House, 2014, 309–335.

5 Science fiction is not as old as fantasy, but it's pretty old. See chapter 2.

6 Shumaker, Robert W., et al. *Animal Tool Behavior: The Use and Manufacture of Tools by Animals*. Baltimore: Johns Hopkins, 2024.

7 Comes from the phrase "horse opera," meaning a Western, and especially a Western that leans heavily into the tropes of Westerns.

8 "Ringworld." Larry Niven Wiki, https://larryniven.fandom.com/wiki/Ringworld. Accessed on December 3, 2024.

9 Dickerson, Kelly. "Some of the trickiest science in 'The Martian' came from the book's biggest fans." Business Insider: October 8, 2015. https://www.businessinsider.com/andy-weir-the-martian-science-crowdsourcing-2015–10,

10 Ibid.

11 "Scientific Inaccuracies." The Martian Wikia. https://the-martian.fandom.com/wiki/Scientific_Inaccuracies. Accessed on December 3, 2024.

12 By this I mean science advanced by means of the scientific method, in which scientists propose testable hypotheses and attempt to

175

falsify them experimentally. See Popper, Karl. *The Logic of Scientific Discovery*. New York: Routledge Classics, 1992, 57–73.

13 In fact, there's an interesting contrast with fantasy literature. Science fiction (at least "hard" science fiction, SF with real science in it) tends to look accurate when written and become inaccurate over time. Fantasy looks false from the outset, with its gorgons and magical transformations and encounters with deity, but the best fantasy proves truer over time.

14 For one recent and fun list, see Chu, E. "37 Breakthrough Technologies from Science Fiction." Science Sensei: December 4, 2024. https://sciencesensei.com/37-breakthrough-technologies-from-science-fiction/.

15 This genre arguably also includes stories about Camelot, a utopia doomed by the wickedness of man, and the New Jerusalem of Revelation 21–22, a utopia made possible by the redemption of mankind.

16 Ben Reinhard, "The Haunting of America: Russell Kirk's Ghostly Fiction." The Imaginative Conservative, October 27, 2023 (accessed on October 29, 2024).

CHAPTER ONE

1 The scholarly term for an image of a man with an erection is "ithyphallic."

2 "Lascaux: cave, Dordogne, France." *Britannica.* https://www.britannica.com/place/Lascaux.

3 "Trois Frères: cave, Ariège, France." *Britannica.* https://www.britannica.com/place/Trois-Freres.

4 Though some interpreters have cast doubt on whether the horns are actually visible in photographs of the Sorcerer.

5 De Santillana, Giorgio and von Dechend, Hertha. *Hamlet's Mill: An Essay Investigating the Origins of Human Knowledge and Its Transmission through Myth*. Boston: David R. Godine, 1969.

6 "Thomas Malory: English writer." *Britannica.* https://www.britannica.com/biography/Thomas-Malory.

7 Ibid.

8 "William Caxton: English printer, translator, and publisher." *Britannica.* https://www.britannica.com/biography/William-Caxton.

9 Deuteronomy 32:8.

10 "Sir John Mandeville: English author." *Britannica*. https://www
.britannica.com/biography/John-Mandeville.

11 "Edmund Spenser: English poet." *Britannica*. https://www.britannica
.com/biography/Edmund-Spenser.

12 The "Blatant Beast," a toothed and many-tongued embodiment of
slander, is my favorite.

13 Spenser seems to have planned for his poem to be twenty-four books
long, illustrating twelve private and twelve public virtues.

14 "Horace Walpole: English author." *Britannica*. https://www.britannica
.com/biography/Horace-Walpole.

15 "The Castle of Otranto: novel by Walpole." *Britannica*. https://www
.britannica.com/topic/The-Castle-of-Otranto.

16 "William Blake: British writer and artist." *Britannica*. https://www
.britannica.com/biography/William-Blake.

17 "Hans Christian Andersen: Danish author." *Britannica*. https://www
.britannica.com/biography/Hans-Christian-Andersen-Danish-author.

18 "George MacDonald: British author." *Britannica*. https://www.britannica
.com/biography/George-Macdonald.

19 "William Morris: British artist and author." *Britannica*. https://www
.britannica.com/biography/William-Morris-British-artist-and-author.

20 "Edward John Moreton Drax Plunkett, 18th baron of Dunsany: Irish
dramatist." *Britannica*. https://www.britannica.com/biography/William
-Morris-British-artist-and-author.

21 "L. Frank Baum: American author." *Britannica*. https://www.britannica
.com/biography/L-Frank-Baum.

22 "T. H. White: British writer." *Britannica*. https://www.britannica.com
/biography/T-H-White.

CHAPTER TWO

1 *Hamlet's Mill*, 176–178.

2 "Lucian: Greek writer." *Britannica*. https://www.britannica.com
/biography/Lucian. *Encyclopedia of Science Fiction*, s.v. "Lucian."

3 "Francis Godwin: English bishop and historian." *Britannica*. https:
//www.britannica.com/biography/Francis-Godwin.

4 In the classic romantic comedy *Roxanne*.

5 "Savinien de Cyrano de Bergerac: French author." *Britannica*. https:
//www.britannica.com/biography/Savinien-Cyrano-de-Bergerac.

6   "Daniel Defoe: English author." *Britannica.* https://www.britannica
    .com/biography/Daniel-Defoe.

7   "Mary Wollstonecraft Shelley: British author." *Britannica.* https://www
    .britannica.com/biography/Mary-Wollstonecraft-Shelley.

8   The title of my middle grade fantasy series, *The Extraordinary
    Journeys of Clockwork Charlie*, is an homage to this fact and to Verne.

9   "Jules Verne: French author." *Britannica.* https://www.britannica.com
    /biography/Jules-Verne.

10 "H. G. Wells: British author." *Britannica.* https://www.britannica.com
    /biography/H-G-Wells. *Encyclopedia of Science Fiction*, s.v. "Wells,
    H(erbert) G(eorge)."

11 "Samuel Butler: British author." *Britannica.* https://www.britannica
    .com/biography/Samuel-Butler-English-author-1835–1902.

12 "Edgar Rice Burroughs: American novelist." *Britannica.* https://www
    .britannica.com/biography/Edgar-Rice-Burroughs. *Encyclopedia of
    Science Fiction*, s.v. "Burroughs, Edgar Rice."

CHAPTER THREE

1   *Encyclopedia of Fantasy*, s.v. "Howard, Robert E(rvin)." *Encyclopedia
    of Science Fiction*, s.v. "Howard, Robert E(rvin)."

2   *Encyclopedia of Fantasy*, s.v. "Lovecraft, H(oward) P(hillips)."
    Encyclopedia of Science Fiction, s.v. "Lovecraft, H(oward) P(hillips)."

3   *Encyclopedia of Science Fiction*, s.v. "Arkham House."

4   Stacy Muth. "October Hall of Fame Inductee – Call of Cthulhu."
    ennie-awards.com. October 26, 2024. Accessed on October 31, 2024.

5   *Encyclopedia of Science Fiction*, s.v. "Asimov, Isaac."

6   Asimov, Isaac. "Runaround". *I, Robot* (The Isaac Asimov Collection
    ed.). New York City: Doubleday, 1950, 40.

7   *Encyclopedia of Science Fiction*, s.v. "Clarke, Arthur C(harles)."

8   Gal, Roy. "An Interstellar Visitor Unmasked." *University of Hawai'i
    News.* November 20, 2017.

9   *Encyclopedia of Science Fiction*, s.v. "Heinlein, Robert A(nson)."

10 Jennifer Weaver, Trademark lawsuit settled between FanX Salt Lake
    Comic Convention, San Diego Comic-Con, kutv.com, July 31, 2020
    (accessed on October 29, 2024).

11 *Encyclopedia of Fantasy*, s.v. "Leiber, Fritz (Reuter Jr.)." *Encyclopedia
    of Science Fiction*, s.v. "Leiber, Fritz (Reuter Jr.)."

CHAPTER FOUR

1 *Encyclopedia of Fantasy*, s.v. "Inklings."

2 "J. R. R. Tolkien: English author." *Britannica*. https://www.britannica .com/biography/J-R-R-Tolkien. *Encyclopedia of Fantasy*, s.v. "Tolkien, J(ohn) R(onald) R(euel)."

3 Shippey, Tom. *J. R. R. Tolkien*. New York: Houghton Mifflin Company, 2000, 174–187.

4 As Shippey himself points out. Ibid, 208.

5 "C. S. Lewis: Irish-born author and scholar." *Britannica*. https://www .britannica.com/biography/C-S-Lewis. *Encyclopedia of Fantasy*, s.v. "Lewis, C(live) S(taples)."

6 *Encyclopedia of Fantasy*, s.v. "Williams, Charles (Walter Stansby)."

7 Gevers, Nick. "Could a former engineer who helped invent Pringles be our greatest living writer?" *The Washington Post*. April 7, 2002.

8 *Encyclopedia of Fantasy*, s.v. "Wolfe, Gene (Rodman)." *Encyclopedia of Science Fiction*, s.v. "Wolfe, Gene (Rodman)."

9 Gordon, Joan. *Gene Wolfe*. Starmont reader's guide (reprint, annotated ed.). Wildside Press LLC, 1986, 96.

CHAPTER FIVE

1 *Encyclopedia of Science Fiction*, s.v. "Bradbury, Ray(mond) (Douglas)."

2 Available at https://www.orwellfoundation.com/the-orwell-foundation /orwell/essays-and-other-works/politics-and-the-english-language/. Accessed on November 1, 2024.

3 "George Orwell: British author." *Britannica*. https://www.britannica .com/biography/George-Orwell. *Encyclopedia of Science Fiction*, s.v. "Orwell, George."

4 "Kurt Vonnegut: American novelist." *Britannica*. https://www.britannica .com/biography/Kurt-Vonnegut. *Encyclopedia of Science Fiction*, s.v. "Vonnegut, Kurt Jr."

5 "Slaughterhouse-Five: novel by Vonnegut." *Britannica*. https://www .britannica.com/topic/Slaughterhouse-Five.

6 "Mervyn Peake: English novelist." *Britannica*. https://www.britannica .com/biography/Mervyn-Peake. *Encyclopedia of Fantasy*, s.v. "Peake, Mervyn (Laurence)"

CHAPTER SIX

1   "Frank Herbert: American author." *Britannica*. https://www.britannica .com/biography/Frank-Herbert. *Encyclopedia of Science Fiction*, s.v. "Herbert, Frank (Patrick)."

2   Moorcock, Michael. "Epic Pooh." In Bloom, Harold (ed.). *Bloom's Modern Critical Interpretation: JRR Tolkien's 'The Lord of the Rings'.* Facts on File, 2008, 3–18.

3   "Michael Moorcock: British author." *Britannica*. https://www.britannica .com/biography/Michael-Moorcock. *Encyclopedia of Fantasy*, s.v. "Moorcock, Michael (John)." *Encyclopedia of Science Fiction*, s.v. "Moorcock, Michael (John)."

4   *Encyclopedia of Fantasy*, s.v. "Zelazny, Roger (Joseph)." *Encyclopedia of Science Fiction*, s.v. "Zelazny, Roger (Joseph)."

5   "Ursula K. Le Guin: American author." *Britannica*. https://www .britannica.com/biography/Ursula-K-Le-Guin. *Encyclopedia of Fantasy*, s.v. "Le Guin, Ursula K(roeber)." *Encyclopedia of Science Fiction*, s.v. "Le Guin, Ursula K(roeber)."

6   "Samuel R. Delany: American author and critic." *Britannica*. https: //www.britannica.com/biography/ Samuel-R-Delany. *Encyclopedia of Fantasy*, s.v. "Delany, Samuel R(ay)." *Encyclopedia of Science Fiction*, s.v. "Delany, Samuel R(ay)."

7   *Encyclopedia of Fantasy*, s.v. "Silverberg, Robert." *Encyclopedia of Science Fiction*, s.v. "Silverberg, Robert."

8   "Philip K. Dick: American author." *Britannica*. https://www.britannica .com/biography/Philip-K-Dick. *Encyclopedia of Science Fiction*, s.v. "Dick, Philip K(indred)."

CHAPTER SEVEN

1   *Encyclopedia of Science Fiction*, s.v. "Niven, Larry."

2   "Nevinyrral." MTG Wiki. https://mtg.fandom.com/wiki/Nevinyrral . Accessed on December 2, 2024.

3   *Encyclopedia of Science Fiction*, s.v. "Pournelle, Jerry E(ugene)."

4   Jerry Pournelle. "Ready Line Overload." *Byte*. February 1989. p. 136.

5   *Encyclopedia of Science Fiction*, s.v. "Anderson, Poul (William)." See also *Encyclopedia of Fantasy*, s.v. "Anderson, Poul (William)."

6   Algis Budrys. "Galaxy Bookshelf." *Galaxy Science Fiction*. February 1965. p. 153.

7   *Encyclopedia of Science Fiction*, s.v. "Bear, Greg."

CHAPTER EIGHT

1   *Encyclopedia of Fantasy*, s.v. "Brooks, Terry."
2   Brooks, Terry (2002) [1991]. "Author's Note to *The Elfstones of Shannara*".
3   *Encyclopedia of Fantasy*, s.v. "Donaldson, Stephen R(eeder)." *Encyclopedia of Science Fiction*, s.v. "Donaldson, Stephen R(eeder)."
4   *Encyclopedia of Fantasy*, s.v. "Cook, Glen (Charles)." *Encyclopedia of Science Fiction*, s.v. "Cook, Glen (Charles)."
5   *Encyclopedia of Fantasy*, s.v. "Anthony, Piers." *Encyclopedia of Science Fiction*, s.v. "Anthony, Piers."
6   *Encyclopedia of Fantasy*, s.v. "Pratchett, Terry." *Encyclopedia of Science Fiction*, s.v. "Pratchett, Terry."
7   *Encyclopedia of Fantasy*, s.v. "Asprin, Robert Lynn." *Encyclopedia of Science Fiction*, s.v. "Asprin, Robert Lynn."
8   *Encyclopedia of Fantasy*, s.v. "Nye, Jody Lynn."
9   *Encyclopedia of Science Fiction*, s.v. "Adams, Douglas (Noel)."

CHAPTER NINE

1   Walker, Martin. "Blade Runner on electro-steroids." *Mail & Guardian*. July 14, 2014.
2   *Encyclopedia of Science Fiction*, s.v. "Gibson, William (Ford)."
3   Andrew Liptak. "The Futurians and the 1939 World Science Fiction Convention." *Kirkus Reviews*. May 9, 2013. Accessed on October 30, 2024.
4   Britt, Aaron. "On Language: Avatar." *New York Times Magazine*. August 10, 2008.

CHAPTER TEN

1   Founders of Steampunk at World Fantasy, K.W. Jeter, Tim Powers, James Blaylock, John Berlyne. YouTube. https://www.youtube.com/watch?v=rrU88-cx7uw.
2   Wilby, Emma. *Cunning Folk and Familiar Spirits: Shamanistic Visionary Traditions in Early Modern British Witchcraft and Magic*. Chicago: Sussex Academic Press, 2005, 3.
3   Jeter, K.W. (April 1987). "Letter—essay from K. W. Jeter". *Locus*. Vol. 20, no. 4. Locus Publications.
4   "Defining Steampunk as an Aesthetic." Retroactive: The Further Adventures of the Steampunk Scholar. May 17, 2010. https:

//steampunkscholar.blogspot.com/2010/05/defining-steampunk-as
-aesthetic.html. Accessed October 25, 2024.

CHAPTER ELEVEN

1   Spring, Kit. "Elf and efficiency." *The Guardian.* January 25, 2004.
2   Ibid.
3   Hat tip to her quite manly son Todd, who has continued the series.
4   Taking their cues from John Norman's *Gor* novels.
5   Adam Whitehead. "It has been revealed that fantasy author David
    Eddings and his wife were jailed in the 1970s for child abuse." The
    Wertzone: SF&F In Print & On Screen. May 2, 2020. Accessed on
    October 30, 2024. It may be worth noting that Eddings became fantasy
    novelists after serving prison time and I am unaware of any allega-
    tion that he abused children subsequently.
6   Allison Flood. "SFF community reeling after Marion Zimmer
    Bradley's daughter accuses her of abuse." *The Guardian.* June 27, 2014.
    Accessed on October 30, 2024.
7   Samuel R. Delany, Queer Desires Forum, New York City, June 25, 1994,
    quoted at https://www.tumblr.com/samueldelany/91784553596/a
    -conversation-with-samuel-r-delany-about-nambla. Accessed on
    October 30, 2024. A blog interview between Delany and blogger Will
    Shetterly about sexuality and consent posted shortly after the accu-
    sations against Marion Zimmer Bradley has been taken down.
8   Paul Caruana Galizia, et al. "Exclusive: Neil Gaiman accused of sex-
    ual assault." *Tortoise.* July 3, 2024. Accessed on October 30, 2024.
9   Meacham, Steve (13 December 2003). "The shed where God died".
    Sydney Morning Herald Online.

CHAPTER TWELVE

1   Rice, Anne. *Christ the Lord: Out of Egypt: A Novel.* New York:
    Ballantine Books, 2008, 323–325.
2   "Mercedes Lackey Removed from Nebula Conference." Locus. May
    23, 2022. Accessed on October 30, 2024.
3   https://mercedeslackeyblog.tumblr.com/post/685121410657566720/i
    -wish-to-apologize. Accessed on October 30, 2024.
4   Salvoni, Elena. "The CHILD assassins as young as ELEVEN carrying
    out machine-gun murders on the streets of Sweden for up to £13,000

a hit . . . and CANNOT be prosecuted." *The Daily Mail*. December 2, 2024.

CHAPTER THIRTEEN

1 *Encyclopedia of Science Fiction*, s.v. "Card, Orson Scott."
2 *Encyclopedia of Science Fiction*, s.v. "Bujold, Lois McMaster."

CHAPTER FOURTEEN

1 John Mauro. "Review: The Wind-Up Bird Chronicle by Haruki Murakami." *Grimdark Magazine*. May 10, 2024. Accessed on October 30, 2024.

CHAPTER FIFTEEN

1 *Liddell and Scott's Greek-English Lexicon*, s.v. "mageia".
2 Matthew 2.
3 Yuval Harari, *Jewish Magic before the Rise of Kabbalah*, Detroit: Wayne State University Press, 2017, pp. 15–67.
4 Ibid p. 15.
5 Ibid p. 20.
6 Ibid p. 18.
7 Ibid pp. 29–30.
8 Ibid p. 53.
9 Ibid pp. 21–23.
10 Ibid p. 18.
11 Ibid pp. 34–45.
12 Ibid pp. 32–33.
13 Ibid pp. 35–38.
14 Ibid p. 38.
15 Ibid p. 58.
16 Ibid p. 63.
17 Ibid p. 64.
18 Ibid p. 65.
19 Ibid p. 65.
20 Ibid p. 24.
21 Ibid pp. 26–28, 39–43.
22 Ibid pp. 45–50.
23 Ibid p. 59.

24 This discussion of the limitations of hard magic was previously published under the title "MAGIC SYSTEMS AREN'T MAGIC: A few initial notes toward more authentic magic in fantasy novels and an invitation to read Witchy Eye" on www.baen.com.

25 *Encyclopedia of Fantasy*, s.v. "Martin, George R(aymond) R(ichard)." *Encyclopedia of Science Fiction*, s.v. "Martin, George R(aymond) R(ichard)."

26 "A Talk with George R.R. Martin." YouTube. https://www.youtube.com/watch?v=OYmJu60OW8E. Accessed on October 25, 2024.

CHAPTER SIXTEEN

1 A version of this chapter was previously published as: Butler, D. J. "The Long Arm Of Chinese Censorship Comes For Science Fiction Awards." *The Federalist*. March 1, 2024.

2 Jason Kehe. "Brandon Sanderson Is Your God: He's the biggest fantasy writer in the world. He's also very Mormon. These things are profoundly related." *Wired*. March 23, 2023. Accessed on October 30, 2024.

CHAPTER SEVENTEEN

1 Weiner, David. "How the Battle for 'Lord of the Rings' Nearly Broke a Director." *The Hollywood Reporter*. November 10, 2018.

CHAPTER EIGHTEEN

1 Jones, Jason B. "Ending The Wheel of Time: The GeekDad Interview with Brandon Sanderson." *Wired*. November 2, 2009.

2 *Encyclopedia of Science Fiction*, s.v. "Robinson, Kim Stanley."

INDEX